Fractions, Decimals and Percentages

Fractions 4

Teacher's Guide

Hilary Koll and Steve Mills

Schofield & Sims

Free downloads available from the Schofield & Sims website

A selection of free downloads is available from the Schofield & Sims website (www.schofieldandsims.co.uk/free-downloads). These may be used to further enhance the effectiveness of the programme. The downloads add to the range of print materials supplied in the teacher's guides.

- **Graphics** slides containing the visual elements from each teacher's guide unit provided as Microsoft PowerPoint® presentations.
- **Go deeper investigations** providing additional extension material to develop problem-solving and reasoning skills.
- **Additional resources** including a fraction wall, a comparison chart and number lines to support learning and teaching.

Published by **Schofield & Sims Ltd**, Dogley Mill, Fenay Bridge, Huddersfield HD8 0NQ, UK
Telephone 01484 607080
www.schofieldandsims.co.uk

This edition copyright © Schofield & Sims Ltd, 2017
First published in 2017

Authors: **Hilary Koll and Steve Mills**
Hilary Koll and Steve Mills have asserted their moral rights under the Copyright, Designs and Patents Act, 1988, to be identified as the authors of this work.

British Library Cataloguing in Publication Data
A catalogue record for this book is available from the British Library.

All rights reserved. Except where otherwise indicated, no part of this publication may be reproduced, stored in a retrieval system, or transmitted in any form or by any means, electronic, mechanical, photocopying, recording or otherwise, without either the prior permission of the publisher or a licence permitting restricted copying in the United Kingdom issued by the Copyright Licensing Agency Limited, Saffron House, 6–10 Kirby Street, London EC1N 8TS.

The **Teacher's notes graphics** and **Assessment resources** are exempt from these restrictions and may be photocopied or scanned after purchase, where indicated, for use within the purchaser's institution only.

All registered trademarks remain the property of their respective holders. Their names are used only to directly describe the products.

Design by **Oxford Designers & Illustrators Ltd**
Printed in the UK by **Page Bros (Norwich) Ltd**

ISBN 978 07217 1382 3

Introduction			4
Teacher's notes	Unit 1	Understand the role of the numerator and denominator	12
	Unit 2	Use fractions in different representations, including sets	14
	Unit 3	Recognise mixed numbers	16
	Unit 4	Find equivalent fractions using a fraction wall	18
	Unit 5	Use patterns within families of equivalent fractions	20
	Unit 6	Add and subtract fractions with the same denominator	22
	Unit 7	Understand tenths as fractions and decimals	24
	Unit 8	Find decimals with one decimal place on a number line	26
	Unit 9	Order and round decimals with one decimal place	28
	Unit 10	Divide one-digit numbers by 10	30
	Unit 11	Divide one- or two-digit numbers by 10	32
	Unit 12	Understand fractions and decimals as the result of division	34
	Unit 13	Recognise hundredths as fractions and decimals	36
	Unit 14	Find decimals with two decimal places on a number line	38
	Unit 15	Compare and order decimals with two decimal places	40
	Unit 16	Divide one- or two-digit numbers by 100	42
	Unit 17	Solve problems, including finding fractions of amounts	44
	Unit 18	Solve problems with money and measures	46
Answers	Unit 1	Understand the role of the numerator and denominator	48
	Unit 2	Use fractions in different representations, including sets	50
	Unit 3	Recognise mixed numbers	52
	Unit 4	Find equivalent fractions using a fraction wall	54
	Unit 5	Use patterns within families of equivalent fractions	56
	Unit 6	Add and subtract fractions with the same denominator	58
	Test	Check-up test 1	60
	Unit 7	Understand tenths as fractions and decimals	62
	Unit 8	Find decimals with one decimal place on a number line	64
	Unit 9	Order and round decimals with one decimal place	66
	Unit 10	Divide one-digit numbers by 10	68
	Unit 11	Divide one- or two-digit numbers by 10	70
	Unit 12	Understand fractions and decimals as the result of division	72
	Test	Check-up test 2	74
	Unit 13	Recognise hundredths as fractions and decimals	76
	Unit 14	Find decimals with two decimal places on a number line	78
	Unit 15	Compare and order decimals with two decimal places	80
	Unit 16	Divide one- or two-digit numbers by 100	82
	Unit 17	Solve problems, including finding fractions of amounts	84
	Unit 18	Solve problems with money and measures	86
	Test	Check-up test 3	88
	Test	Final test	90
Assessment	Pupil progress chart		94
	Final test group record sheet		95

Overview

Fractions, decimals and percentages are frequent areas of difficulty in mathematics for primary school pupils. Many teachers find them challenging to teach and pupils often have limited or only partially developed conceptual understanding of the topics. A major reason children struggle with fractions, decimals and percentages is the variety of contexts and representations in which they appear – for example, as areas, as sets, on number lines, as a result of a division problem and in relation to measurements.

Schofield & Sims Fractions, Decimals and Percentages is a structured whole-school programme designed to help pupils develop a deep, secure and adaptable understanding of these topics. The series consists of six pupil books and six teacher's guides, one for each primary school year.

Each unit of the programme addresses a single learning objective. The teacher's guides provide detailed teaching notes with accompanying graphics to use in lessons. The pupil books provide a summary of the learning objective and a set of related practice questions that increase in difficulty. This allows you, the teacher or adult helper, to introduce and teach a particular concept and then to provide appropriate intelligent practice which gradually leads children towards more complex representations and varied contexts.

Supporting a mastery approach, all pupils are encouraged to move at the same pace through the units and are given the same opportunity to fully understand the concept being taught. Depth of learning is emphasised over speed of learning and the pupils should have a solid understanding of the content of each unit before moving on to new material. Downloadable **Go deeper** extension resources help to cement pupils' understanding of the concepts that have been taught. The series also provides ongoing and integrated assessment throughout.

Fractions 4 and the National Curriculum

Fractions 4 and its related **Teacher's Guide** match the statutory requirements for Year 4 for 'Fractions (including decimals)' in the National Curriculum. The 10 statutory requirements are listed below. They have been coded for ease of reference. For example, Y4/F1 refers to the first fractions requirement in Year 4.

National Curriculum requirements for 'Fractions (including decimals)'

Y4/F1 Recognise and show, using diagrams, families of common equivalent fractions.

Y4/F2 Count up and down in hundredths; recognise that hundredths arise when dividing an object by one hundred and dividing tenths by ten.

Y4/F3 Solve problems involving increasingly harder fractions to calculate quantities, and fractions to divide quantities, including non-unit fractions where the answer is a whole number.

Y4/F4 Add and subtract fractions with the same denominator.

Y4/F5 Recognise and write decimal equivalents of any number of tenths or hundredths.

Y4/F6 Recognise and write decimal equivalents to $\frac{1}{4}, \frac{1}{2}, \frac{3}{4}$.

Y4/F7 Find the effect of dividing a one- or two-digit number by 10 and 100, identifying the value of the digits in the answer as ones, tenths and hundredths.

Y4/F8 Round decimals with one decimal place to the nearest whole number.

Y4/F9 Compare numbers with the same number of decimal places up to two decimal places.

Y4/F10 Solve simple measure and money problems involving fractions and decimals to two decimal places.

National Curriculum coverage chart

This chart maps all the units and tests in **Fractions 4** against the National Curriculum requirements. When reading the chart, please refer to the curriculum coding introduced on page 4. The light shaded boxes show where a requirement is touched upon and the dark shaded boxes show the key units and tests for that requirement.

	Y3 Revision	Y4/F1	Y4/F2	Y4/F3	Y4/F4	Y4/F5	Y4/F6	Y4/F7	Y4/F8	Y4/F9	Y4/F10
Unit 1	D				L						D
Unit 2	D	L		L							D
Unit 3	D				L						
Unit 4		D									
Unit 5		D									
Unit 6					D						
Check-up test 1		D			D						D
Unit 7					L	D	D	D		L	D
Unit 8						D	L			L	D
Unit 9						D	L		D	D	D
Unit 10		L		L				D			D
Unit 11		L		L		L					
Unit 12		L		D							
Check-up test 2				D		D	D	D	D	D	D
Unit 13		D	D			D	D			L	D
Unit 14		L				D				L	D
Unit 15				D						D	D
Unit 16				D				D			L
Unit 17					D						
Unit 18		L		D			D				L
Check-up test 3				D			D		D	D	D
Final test		L	L	L	L	L	L	L	L	L	L

Prerequisites for Fractions 4

Before beginning **Fractions 4** the pupils should have an understanding of both unit and non-unit fractions. Each year of the programme, however, begins with revision to ensure that the pupils understand the necessary ideas to move forward. The first column in the chart on page 5, labelled 'Y3 Revision', shows the units that revise Year 3 material. The pupils can be given **Fractions 3** first if they require further practice to build their confidence and their understanding.

The focus in Year 4 is on the following areas: families of equivalent fractions, counting in hundredths, dividing one- and two-digit numbers by ten or one hundred, simple decimal equivalents, rounding decimals to the nearest whole number, comparing decimals with up to two decimal places, and problem solving.

Fractions 4 Teacher's Guide

The **Fractions 4 Teacher's Guide** contains everything you need to teach the National Curriculum requirements for 'Fractions' in Year 4. There are 18 corresponding units in the teacher's guide and pupil book, six for each term.

Using the Teacher's notes

In this teacher's guide you will find **Teacher's notes** for each unit (pages 12 to 47). These include a detailed lesson plan with accompanying graphics that can be used to demonstrate the learning objective before the pupils begin the activities in the pupil book. The graphics are visual prompts for the class and can be used in a variety of ways. They are all available as interactive PowerPoint® presentations (free to download from the Schofield & Sims website). Alternatively, the graphics could be presented on a projector, or photocopied and used as pupil handouts, or used as a guide when drawing your own visual prompts. The lesson plans can be easily adapted to suit your classroom. Below is an example lesson from this teacher's guide, alongside the corresponding slides from the **Fractions 4** Powerpoint® presentation.

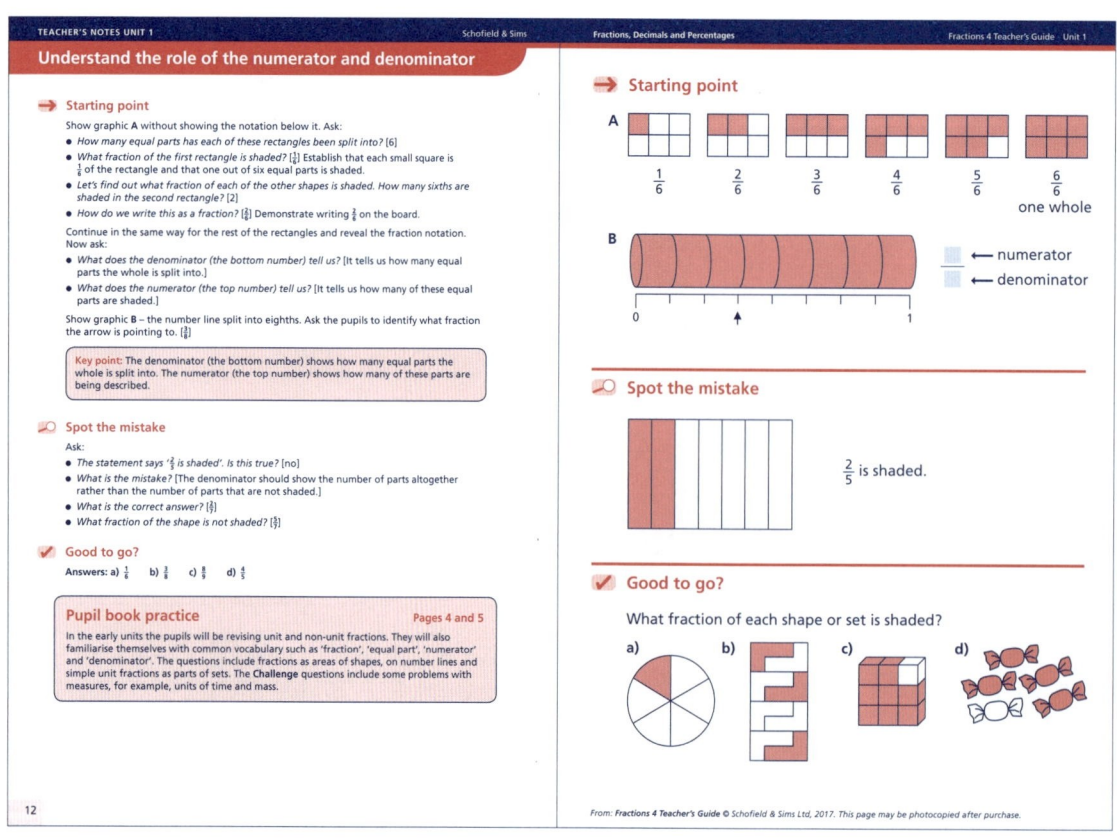

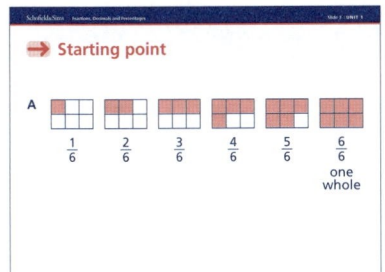 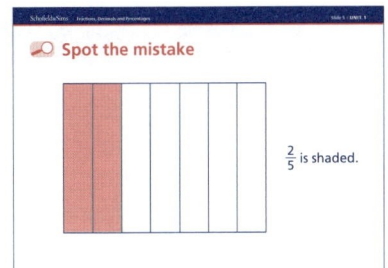 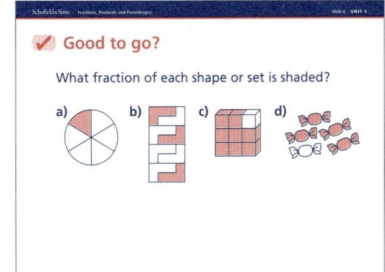

The **Teacher's notes** for each unit are divided into the following sections:

- **Starting point** – This section provides clear instruction on how to introduce and teach the learning objective. Using the graphics as prompts, probing questions are given that draw on the pupils' prior knowledge and encourage them to find connections, reason and reach conclusions about why the concept being taught is true. The **Key point** of the lesson is clearly highlighted.

- **Spot the mistake** – This is a statement, often with a visual element, that represents a mistake which is commonly made with the concept being taught. The statement is intentionally incorrect. You are given a series of corrective questions to ask the pupils, drawing out potential misconceptions and helping them to spot the mistake. Procedural understanding is deepened as the pupils discuss why the statement is incorrect and what the correct statement should be.

- **Good to go?** – This section has quick practice questions that help you establish whether each pupil has understood the lesson and is a useful tool for formative assessment. It is suggested that the pupils answer these questions on mini-whiteboards and hold up their answers. This helps you to quickly identify the pupils who require further assistance and those who have fully understood the unit focus.

- **Pupil book practice** – This section provides links to the pupil book pages for this unit. It flags potential areas of difficulty to be aware of in the activities, highlights when questions act as a bridge to later units, and offers further suggestions for practical resources you can use to support the pupils as they work.

Answers

The teacher's guide contains a complete set of **Answers** (pages 48 to 93) for all the units and tests in the pupil book. The answers are presented as correctly completed pupil book pages to make marking quick and easy.

Fractions 4 Pupil Book

Once you are confident that the pupils have grasped the concept of the lesson, they should turn to the corresponding unit in their pupil book. This offers varied activities of increasing difficulty that provide plenty of repetition, practice and challenge to consolidate learning.

The pupil book begins with a simple introduction which clearly explains the purpose of the book and how it is used. This introduction supports your own instructions for the pupils as they start this book. It is also a useful reference for parents if you decide to set sections of the pupil book as homework. On the following page is an example lesson from the pupil book.

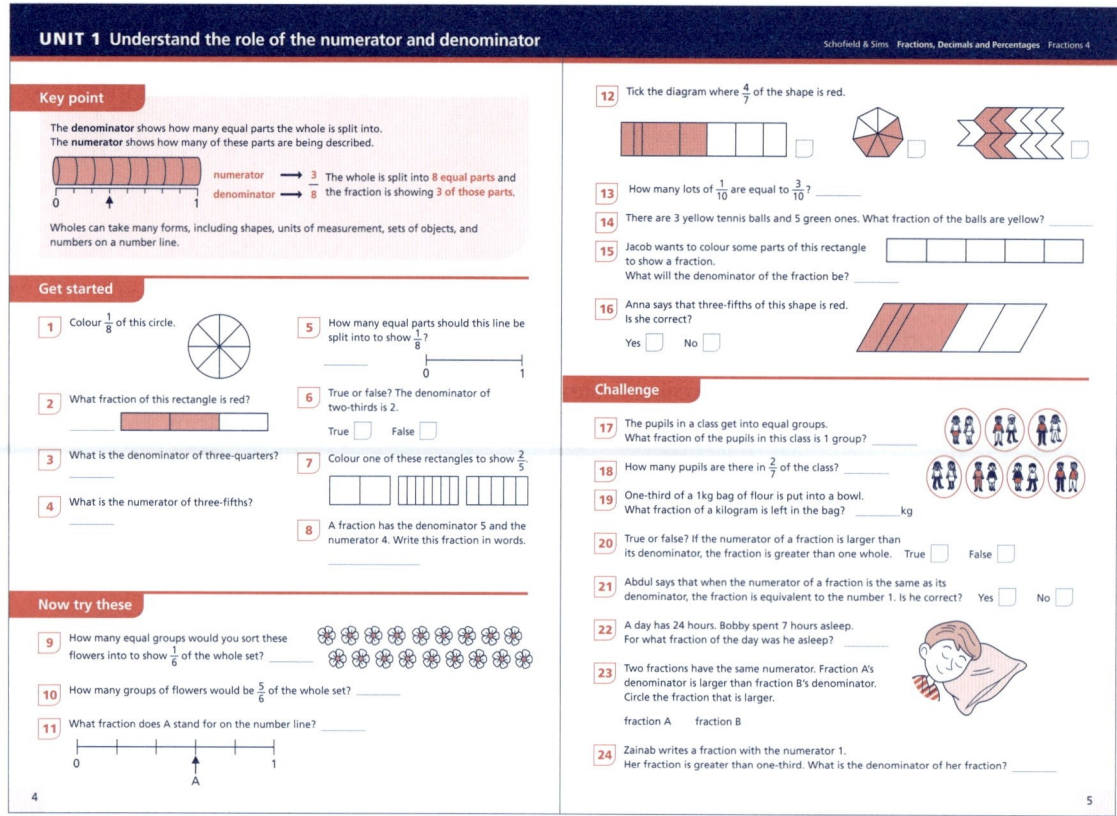

Each unit in the pupil book begins with a child-friendly summary of the **Key point** of the lesson, as a reminder for the pupil and to assist parents in supporting their children at home.

The practice questions in each unit are divided into three sections.

- **Get started** – Quick questions to help the pupil gain confidence in the topic, with a variety of straightforward practice questions related to the learning objective.

- **Now try these** – Additional number and practical problems to take the topic further with more varied vocabulary and representations.

- **Challenge** – Problem-solving questions involving greater challenge such as measurement and money contexts and links to other more complex concepts.

The pupils should write their answers directly into their own pupil book. Each completed pupil book provides a permanent record of achievement and encourages the pupils to take pride in their work. Three **Check-up tests**, one for the end of each term, a **Final test** and a **How did I find it?** checklist are also included in each pupil book. These help you to monitor the pupils' progress.

> **Strategies for learning**
>
> If a pupil is struggling with a question, prompt them to try it again using a different strategy. Problem-solving strategies develop deeper mathematical thinking, allowing pupils to solve a wider variety of problems.
>
> - **Visualising** – *Sketch a picture of the situation or use real-life objects to model it.*
> - **Simplifying** – *If a problem seems too difficult, make it easier. For example, change decimals into whole numbers, and work out how you would solve the easier problem. Then go back to the harder problem and see if you can find the answer.*
> - **Using trial and improvement** – *It can help to guess what the answer might be. Look at the question again, with the guessed number in mind, and see how your guess needs to be changed. Sometimes you can get an idea of whether the answer is larger or smaller than your guess. Choose an adjusted number and keep repeating this until you get to the right answer.*
> - **Reasoning** – *Discuss the problem with a partner and make suggestions such as 'If you tried adding, would that work?' or 'Do you think dividing would give us the answer?'. Suggestions don't have to be right but they can really help to get you thinking.*
> - **Looking for patterns** – *Look out for patterns in the numbers in a problem. Sometimes you can find an answer by spotting a pattern and continuing it.*
> - **Generalising** – *Some problems involve thinking of an idea more generally or saying whether a statement is never, sometimes or always true. For this you must generalise. This means thinking carefully about an idea in lots of different situations.*
> - **Checking** – *Go back and check your answers. You could use inverse operations or work backwards from the answer. Make sure you haven't made any wrong assumptions.*
> - **Persevering** – *When all else fails, keep going! Try using a coloured pen to highlight the important numbers in the problem and see if that helps you to spot a pattern.*

Go deeper

When teaching for mastery, differentiation is achieved by emphasising depth of knowledge and mathematical fluency over pace of learning. The **Challenge** questions in the pupil book offer sophisticated problems that will stretch even the more able student and provide the practice that is required to exceed the expected national standards. **Go deeper investigations** are also available (free to download from the Schofield & Sims website), which correspond with the content covered up to each **Check-up test**. These group work problem-solving activities help pupils to delve more deeply into the concepts being taught and cement their understanding. Teacher's notes and pupil worksheets are provided for each investigation. These can be used with the whole class in a dedicated problem-solving lesson or as extension material for pupils who require further challenge.

Assessment

Fractions 4 and its related **Teacher's Guide** offer frequent opportunities and multiple resources for in-school assessment. These resources should be used in line with your school's own assessment policy.

Formative assessment

The teacher's guide lesson plans all feature precise questioning. This can be used as part of your ongoing formative assessment to test the pupils' conceptual and procedural knowledge. The questions can help to uncover a pupil's reasoning and depth of mathematical thinking. The **Good to go?** section at the end of each lesson provides a further check, enabling you to easily identify when pupils are struggling and when they are ready to progress to the pupil book practice questions.

The pupil book units can also be used as a basis for formative assessment. Teachers should monitor the progress that each pupil is making as they work through the pupil book questions. If an answer is incorrect, asking the pupil to explain how they reached this answer may reveal gaps in understanding that can then be addressed.

Three **Check-up tests** are provided in the pupil book. These can be used to test the pupils' understanding of the material covered in the preceding six units. This allows you to ascertain how well the pupils have remembered the ideas covered in the programme so far and how secure their understanding is.

Each pupil's day-to-day progress can be monitored by using the **Pupil progress chart** (at the back of this book). This chart can be photocopied for each pupil in your class so that you can keep track of the marks scored on each unit and **Check-up test**. Guidance is provided below on how to interpret the information gained from the **Pupil progress chart**.

Decoding the unit scores

While the total score achieved in each pupil book unit will be a good indicator of the pupils' overall progress, it is advisable to keep an eye out for patterns in their scores across the three different sections as well.

- If a pupil struggles with **Get started**, it can indicate that the pupil has not yet understood or has misunderstood the concept of the unit and is likely to require further support.

- If a pupil struggles with **Now try these** after a successful **Get started**, it can indicate that the pupil has understood the initial idea but is having trouble applying it to different contexts and with different representations.

- If a pupil struggles with **Challenge** after a successful **Get started** and **Now try these**, it can indicate that the pupil may need further help in problem-solving processes such as reasoning, simplifying, visualising, looking for patterns or generalising. It may also indicate that the pupil is having difficulty with comprehension skills, misunderstanding the language that is used in the question.

- If the pupil is able to make a good attempt at **Challenge** after a successful **Get started** and **Now try these**, it can indicate that the pupil has mastered the unit and is secure in their understanding of the concepts that have been taught.

- If the pupil scores highly across all three sections, it can indicate that the pupil has mastered the concepts of the unit at greater depth.

- Look out for inconsistent scoring across the sections, for example, a low score in **Get started** and a high score in **Now try these** or a low score in **Now try these** and a high score in **Challenge** as this may mean that there are gaps in the pupil's understanding. Some guesswork may have been involved in gaining correct answers.

Decoding the Check-up test scores

- A score of 0–14 can indicate that the pupil has not yet understood all of the key concepts in the preceding units. Further consolidation work or a different approach may be needed to ensure secure understanding.

- A score of 15–20 can indicate that the pupil has mastered the concepts of the preceding units and can confidently move forward.

Each pupil book also contains a **How did I find it?** checklist which enables the pupils to evaluate their own progress as they work through the programme. Each unit has a corresponding 'I can' statement. After completing each unit, **Check-up test** and **Final test** the pupils should be given the opportunity to rate how they found the unit – 'difficult', 'getting there' or 'easy'.

Summative assessment

The **Final test** in the pupil book can be used for in-school summative assessment at the end of **Fractions 4**. This test allows you to assess the pupils' understanding of all the concepts covered in **Fractions 4**. The **Final test** is organised so that each section tests a different statutory requirement for the Year 4 National Curriculum.

Marks for the **Final test** can be recorded on the **Final test group record sheet** (at the back of this book). Record each mark by either ticking or shading the relevant boxes next to each pupil's name. This chart outlines which curriculum requirement is being tested in each section using the curriculum coding that was introduced on page 4. It provides an at-a-glance overview of how the whole class is performing in relation to the National Curriculum requirements and enables you to evaluate pupil learning at the end of the year. Guidance is provided below on how to interpret the information gained from this chart.

> **Decoding the Final test scores**
>
> - A score of 0–22 marks can indicate that the pupil has not fully mastered the key concepts for the year. The curriculum coding should provide a clear idea of which requirements the pupil is struggling with. Catch-up work is likely to be needed in these areas before the pupil is ready to proceed with Year 5 material.
>
> - A score of 23–30 marks can indicate that the pupil has mastered the key concepts for the year and can confidently move forward to Year 5 material. The curriculum coding should provide a clear idea of the pupil's strengths and warn of any areas of weakness that may require additional practice in Year 5.

The **Final test group record sheet** provides a useful record for school leaders and inspectors and will show the subsequent teacher how secure each pupil was in their knowledge of the previous year's curriculum and how ready they are for progression.

➡ Starting point

Show graphic **A** without showing the notation below it. Ask:

- *How many equal parts has each of these rectangles been split into?* [6]
- *What fraction of the first rectangle is shaded?* [$\frac{1}{6}$] Establish that each small square is $\frac{1}{6}$ of the rectangle and that one out of six equal parts is shaded.
- *Let's find out what fraction of each of the other shapes is shaded. How many sixths are shaded in the second rectangle?* [2]
- *How do we write this as a fraction?* [$\frac{2}{6}$] Demonstrate writing $\frac{2}{6}$ on the board.

Continue in the same way for the rest of the rectangles and reveal the fraction notation. Now ask:

- *What does the denominator (the bottom number) tell us?* [It tells us how many equal parts the whole is split into.]
- *What does the numerator (the top number) tell us?* [It tells us how many of these equal parts are shaded.]

Show graphic **B** – the number line split into eighths. Ask the pupils to identify what fraction the arrow is pointing to. [$\frac{3}{8}$]

> **Key point:** The denominator (the bottom number) shows how many equal parts the whole is split into. The numerator (the top number) shows how many of these parts are being described.

🔍 Spot the mistake

Ask:

- *The statement says '$\frac{2}{5}$ is shaded'. Is this true?* [no]
- *What is the mistake?* [The denominator should show the number of parts altogether rather than the number of parts that are not shaded.]
- *What is the correct answer?* [$\frac{2}{7}$]
- *What fraction of the shape is not shaded?* [$\frac{5}{7}$]

✔ Good to go?

Answers: a) $\frac{1}{6}$ b) $\frac{3}{8}$ c) $\frac{8}{9}$ d) $\frac{4}{5}$

> ### Pupil book practice   Pages 4 and 5
>
> In the early units the pupils will be revising unit and non-unit fractions. They will also familiarise themselves with common vocabulary such as 'fraction', 'equal part', 'numerator' and 'denominator'. The questions include fractions as areas of shapes, on number lines and simple unit fractions as parts of sets. The **Challenge** questions include some problems with measures, for example, units of time and mass.

Starting point

A

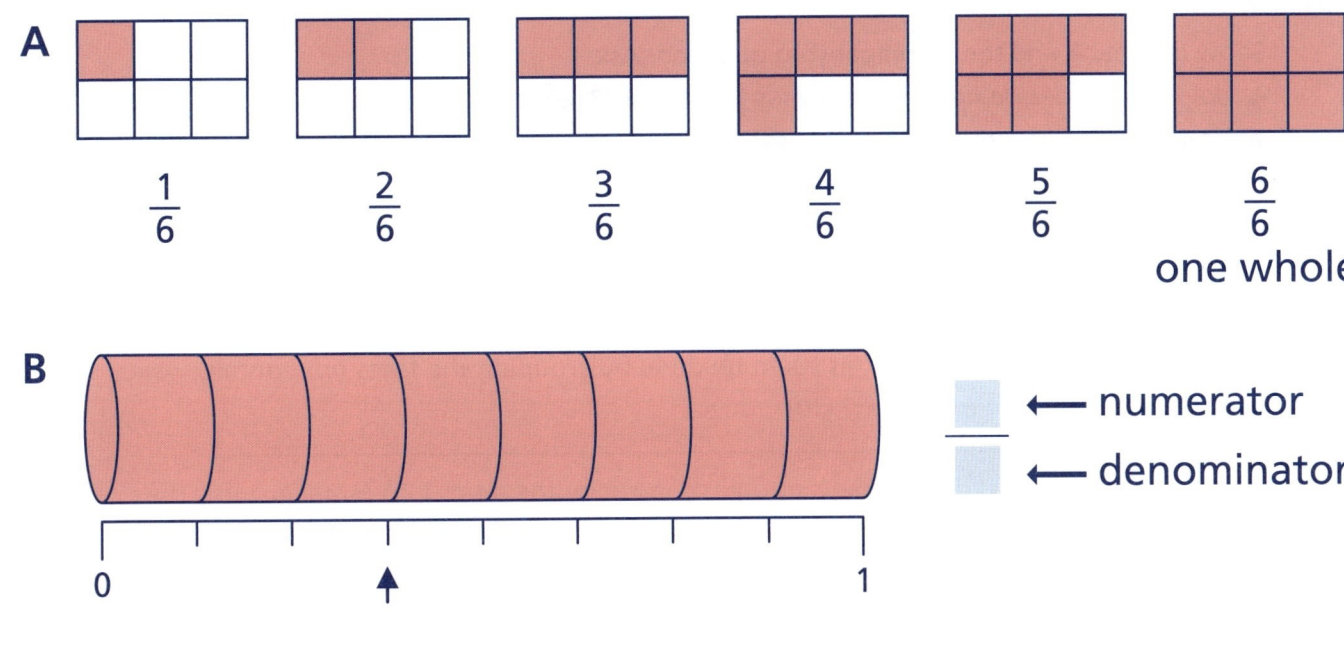

B

Spot the mistake

$\frac{2}{5}$ is shaded.

Good to go?

What fraction of each shape or set is shaded?

a) 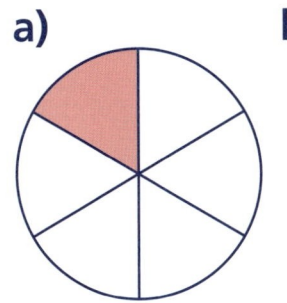   b) 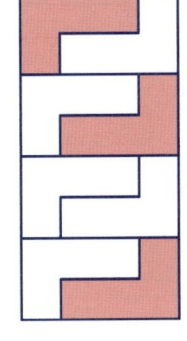   c) 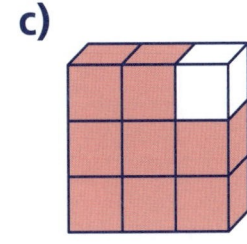   d)

From: Fractions 4 Teacher's Guide © Schofield & Sims Ltd, 2017. This page may be photocopied after purchase.

➡️ Starting point

Show graphic **A** and the accompanying question. Ask:
- *How can we decide how many faces is $\frac{4}{5}$ of the set?* [arrange the faces into equal groups]
- *How many equal groups would we split the set into to show fifths?* [5]

Reveal graphic **B** where the faces have been grouped. Ask:
- *If each group of 3 is $\frac{1}{5}$, how many faces is $\frac{4}{5}$?* [12]
- *If we had to find $\frac{2}{3}$ of the same set of faces, how many equal groups would we split them into?* [3]

Display graphic **C** to show how this could be done by grouping the faces horizontally. Ask:
- *How many faces is $\frac{2}{3}$ of this set?* [10]

> **Key point:** To find fractions of sets of objects, arrange the items into equal groups. The total number of equal groups is shown by the denominator. The number of groups that are needed is shown by the numerator. Count the number of objects in these groups to find the answer.

🔍 Spot the mistake

Ask:
- *The statement says '$\frac{5}{6}$ of these 18 cubes is 12 cubes'. Is this true?* [no]
- *What is the mistake?* [The cubes have been grouped into six equal groups, but only four rather than five of the groups have been counted.]
- *So what is the correct answer?* [15 cubes]

✓ Good to go?

Answers: a) 5   **b)** 15   **c)** 4   **d)** 12

> ### Pupil book practice   Pages 6 and 7
>
> This unit provides further revision of the work covered in **Fractions 3**, to ensure that the pupils are familiar with the many different representations of fractions and, in particular, fractions as parts of sets of objects and arrays. Note which types of representations the pupils struggle with most. If they need further support, return to the related page in **Fractions 3** for more targeted practice. Some pupils may find practical equipment useful for helping them to visualise or group objects when finding fractions. The **Challenge** questions include measurement and money questions such as using centimetres and pounds.

Starting point

How many faces is $\frac{4}{5}$ of this set?

B

15 grouped into fifths

$\frac{1}{5}$ = 3 faces

$\frac{4}{5}$ = 3 × 4 = 12 faces

C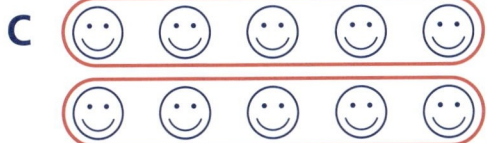

15 grouped into thirds

$\frac{1}{3}$ = 5 faces

$\frac{2}{3}$ = 5 × 2 = 10 faces

Spot the mistake

$\frac{5}{6}$ of these 18 cubes is 12 cubes.

Good to go?

For these 20 squares, find how many squares is:

a) $\frac{1}{4}$ b) $\frac{3}{4}$ c) $\frac{1}{5}$ d) $\frac{3}{5}$

➡ Starting point

Display graphic **A**. Ask:

- *How many equal parts is each whole on this number line divided into?* [5] Draw the pupils' attention to the fact that there are four marks between 6 and 7 on the line but that this represents five intervals, as shown by the shaded areas above the line. Revise counting on in fifths from 6 to 8.

Show number line **B** and ask:

- *What about this number line? How many is each whole split into?* [10] Explain that a number that includes both a whole number and a fraction, such as $7\frac{3}{10}$, is called a 'mixed number'. Point to some positions on the number line and encourage the pupils to say each as a mixed number, for example, $7\frac{4}{10}$ or $8\frac{6}{10}$.

Show the mixed numbers in graphic **C** and ask:

- *Which is the largest of these mixed numbers?* [$7\frac{1}{2}$]
- *How can you tell?* Explain that you can compare them initially by looking at the whole number part. Gradually sort them into order from smallest to largest. [$5\frac{1}{4}$, $5\frac{3}{4}$, $6\frac{1}{2}$, $6\frac{3}{4}$, $7\frac{1}{2}$]

> **Key point:** Mixed numbers are numbers with a whole number and a fraction, such as $4\frac{1}{2}$, $8\frac{3}{4}$ and $5\frac{4}{5}$. Each whole on a number line can be split into any number of equal parts. When counting how many equal parts, be careful to count the intervals.

🔍 Spot the mistake

Ask:

- *In this statement, what is added to $2\frac{3}{5}$?* [1]
- *If you add 1 whole to the mixed number, is the answer $2\frac{4}{5}$?* [no]
- *Why not?* [because you are adding 1 whole not $\frac{1}{5}$]
- *What should the answer be?* [$3\frac{3}{5}$]
- *Why?* [because a mixed number is a whole number and a fraction, so you only need to add 1 to the whole number part: 2 + 1 = 3. The fraction does not change.]

✓ Good to go?

Answers: A = $3\frac{2}{3}$ B = $4\frac{1}{3}$ C = $8\frac{7}{8}$ D = $9\frac{3}{8}$

> ### Pupil book practice   Pages 8 and 9
> These questions offer opportunities for the pupils to identify mixed numbers on number lines and to begin to compare and order them. If the pupils struggle to correctly identify the number of intervals, encourage them to colour each interval as they count it. Questions also involve counting on or back on number lines and linking this to addition and subtraction of simple mixed numbers, wholes and fractions.

Starting point

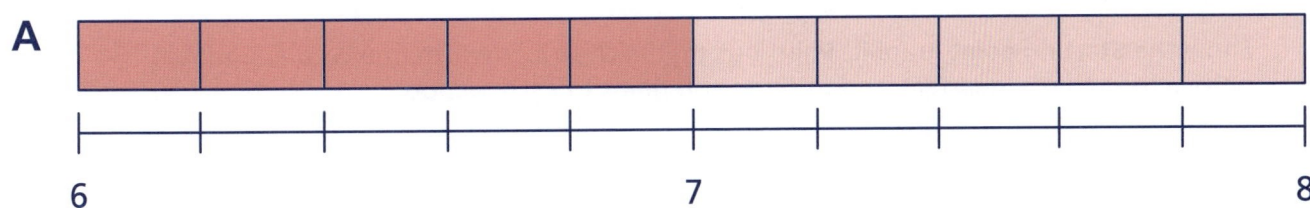

C $6\frac{3}{4}$ $7\frac{1}{2}$ $5\frac{1}{4}$ $6\frac{1}{2}$ $5\frac{3}{4}$

Spot the mistake

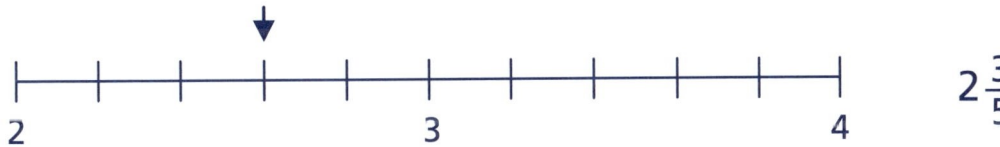

$2\frac{3}{5} + 1 = 2\frac{4}{5}$

Good to go?

What number does each letter show?

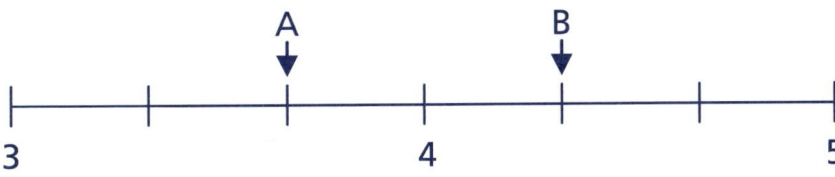

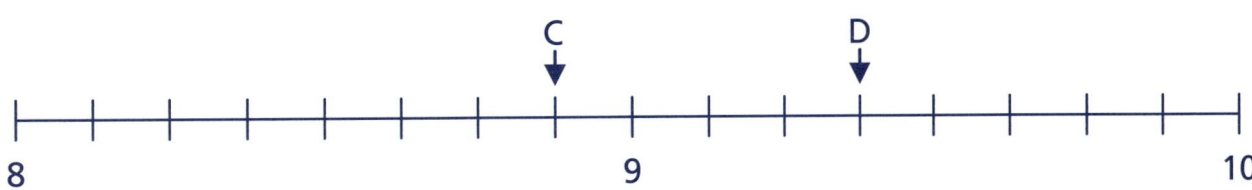

Starting point

Show the **Starting point** graphic. Point out that each strip is worth one whole. Count in halves, then thirds, quarters, and so on as you point to each section of the fraction wall.

Ask:

- *What does it mean when we say two or more fractions are equivalent?* [It means that the fractions have the same value.]
- *How can we find equivalent fractions on this fraction wall?* Demonstrate how to find fractions that line up on the fraction wall by shading $\frac{1}{4}$ and $\frac{2}{8}$ and showing that they are the same amount.

Ask:

- *What fractions on the wall are equivalent to $\frac{2}{3}$?* [$\frac{4}{6}$, $\frac{6}{9}$ and $\frac{8}{12}$] Explain that a group of equivalent fractions is sometimes called 'a family'.
- *What fractions on the wall are equivalent to $\frac{9}{12}$?* [$\frac{3}{4}$ and $\frac{6}{8}$] Encourage the pupils to use a ruler to check accurately.

> **Key point:** Fractions that stand for the same amount are called 'equivalent fractions'. Fraction walls can be used to find equivalent fractions or fraction families.

Spot the mistake

Ask:

- *The statement says '$\frac{3}{5}$ is equivalent to $\frac{8}{10}$'. Is this true?* [no]
- *How can we check?* [Use the fraction wall to show that $\frac{3}{5}$ is equivalent to $\frac{6}{10}$ and that $\frac{4}{5}$ is equivalent to $\frac{8}{10}$.]

Note that a number of pupils may have some knowledge of finding equivalent fractions by multiplying the numerator and denominator by the same number. Encourage them to describe this to the class as a means of checking and explain that the next unit will look at this idea in more detail.

Good to go?

Answers: a) $\frac{2}{6}$, $\frac{3}{9}$, $\frac{4}{12}$ b) $\frac{1}{2}$, $\frac{2}{4}$, $\frac{3}{6}$, $\frac{5}{10}$, $\frac{6}{12}$ c) $\frac{2}{3}$, $\frac{4}{6}$, $\frac{8}{12}$ d) $\frac{3}{4}$, $\frac{9}{12}$

Other equivalent fractions are acceptable.

> ## Pupil book practice   Pages 10 and 11
>
> The **Get Started** section involves questions that can be answered using the fraction wall. (You can download a larger copy from the Schofield & Sims website.) The later sections include fractions shown in different representations that require the pupils to visualise fractions. The last two questions of the **Challenge** section begin to acknowledge the idea that equivalent fractions can be found by multiplying the numerator and denominator by the same number – the following unit explores this in more detail.

Starting point

1											
$\frac{1}{2}$						$\frac{1}{2}$					
$\frac{1}{3}$				$\frac{1}{3}$				$\frac{1}{3}$			
$\frac{1}{4}$			$\frac{1}{4}$			$\frac{1}{4}$			$\frac{1}{4}$		
$\frac{1}{5}$		$\frac{1}{5}$		$\frac{1}{5}$			$\frac{1}{5}$		$\frac{1}{5}$		
$\frac{1}{6}$		$\frac{1}{6}$		$\frac{1}{6}$		$\frac{1}{6}$		$\frac{1}{6}$		$\frac{1}{6}$	
$\frac{1}{7}$		$\frac{1}{7}$		$\frac{1}{7}$		$\frac{1}{7}$		$\frac{1}{7}$		$\frac{1}{7}$	$\frac{1}{7}$
$\frac{1}{8}$	$\frac{1}{8}$	$\frac{1}{8}$	$\frac{1}{8}$	$\frac{1}{8}$	$\frac{1}{8}$	$\frac{1}{8}$	$\frac{1}{8}$				
$\frac{1}{9}$	$\frac{1}{9}$	$\frac{1}{9}$	$\frac{1}{9}$	$\frac{1}{9}$	$\frac{1}{9}$	$\frac{1}{9}$	$\frac{1}{9}$	$\frac{1}{9}$			
$\frac{1}{10}$	$\frac{1}{10}$	$\frac{1}{10}$	$\frac{1}{10}$	$\frac{1}{10}$	$\frac{1}{10}$	$\frac{1}{10}$	$\frac{1}{10}$	$\frac{1}{10}$	$\frac{1}{10}$		
$\frac{1}{11}$	$\frac{1}{11}$	$\frac{1}{11}$	$\frac{1}{11}$	$\frac{1}{11}$	$\frac{1}{11}$	$\frac{1}{11}$	$\frac{1}{11}$	$\frac{1}{11}$	$\frac{1}{11}$	$\frac{1}{11}$	
$\frac{1}{12}$	$\frac{1}{12}$	$\frac{1}{12}$	$\frac{1}{12}$	$\frac{1}{12}$	$\frac{1}{12}$	$\frac{1}{12}$	$\frac{1}{12}$	$\frac{1}{12}$	$\frac{1}{12}$	$\frac{1}{12}$	$\frac{1}{12}$

Spot the mistake

$\frac{3}{5}$ is equivalent to $\frac{8}{10}$.

Good to go?

Write at least two equivalent fractions for each fraction.

a) $\frac{1}{3}$ b) $\frac{4}{8}$ c) $\frac{6}{9}$ d) $\frac{6}{8}$

From: Fractions 4 Teacher's Guide © Schofield & Sims Ltd, 2017. This page may be photocopied after purchase.

Starting point

Show graphic **A** with the fraction notation beneath. Ask:
- *Are these fractions equivalent?* [yes]
- *How do you know?* Discuss that each diagram shows half a rectangle shaded and therefore the fractions are equivalent fractions.

Explain that there is another way to check. If both the numerator and denominator of a fraction are multiplied or divided by the same number, it will always produce an equivalent fraction.

Reveal graphic **B**. Ask:
- *Can you see how the top and bottom of the fraction $\frac{2}{4}$ can be multiplied by 2 to give the fraction $\frac{4}{8}$?*

Look at the next two equivalent fractions in the same way. Ask:
- *Do you see how the top and bottom number is divided by 4 to give $\frac{1}{2}$?*
- *By what number can we multiply both the top and bottom number of $\frac{1}{2}$ to give $\frac{3}{6}$?* [3]

Ensure the pupils understand that both numbers must be multiplied or divided by the same number but that the value of the fraction itself does not change.

Show graphic **C** and ask:
- *What is the missing number?* [9]
- *And so what fraction is equivalent to $\frac{2}{3}$?* [$\frac{6}{9}$]

> **Key point:** If both the numerator and denominator of a fraction are multiplied or divided by the same number, it will always produce an equivalent fraction.

Spot the mistake

Ask:
- *The statement says '$\frac{8}{12} = \frac{2}{4}$'. Is this true?* [no]
- *How can we check this?* [Work out what the first numerator has been divided by to get the second numerator and then see if the denominator has been divided by the same number.]
- *What has the numerator been divided by?* [4]
- *What has the denominator been divided by?* [3]
- *Are these the same?* [no] *So are the two fractions equivalent?* [no]
- *If we divide the denominator by 4 rather than 3, so that both the numerator and denominator are divided by the same number, what equivalent fraction do we get?* [$\frac{2}{3}$]

Good to go?

Answers: a) 8   b) 3   c) 4

> ## Pupil book practice   Pages 12 and 13
>
> Pupils often find it hard to grasp that fractions written with different numbers have the same value as each other and that multiplying or dividing both numbers leaves the value unchanged. If the pupils find these ideas too difficult, again provide them with fraction walls and encourage them to use diagrams to solve the problems. It is not necessary for Year 4 pupils to master the more abstract processes at this stage but, if they can manage it, it is a useful way for them to check their work and gain confidence with equivalence.

Starting point

A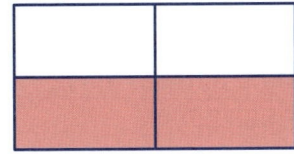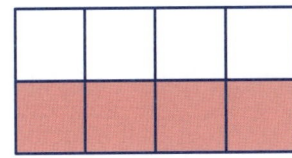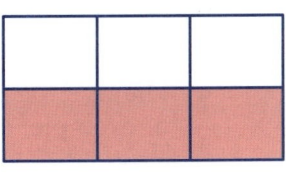

$\frac{2}{4}$ $\frac{4}{8}$ $\frac{1}{2}$ $\frac{3}{6}$

B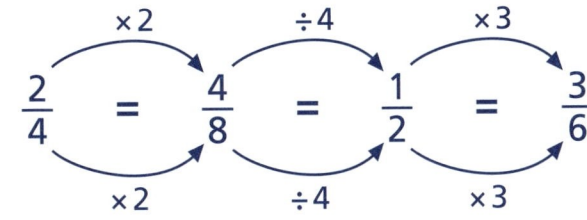

C

$\frac{2}{3} = \frac{6}{\square}$ (×3)

Spot the mistake

$\frac{8}{12} = \frac{2}{4}$

Good to go?

Can you find the missing number in each fraction?

a) $\frac{4}{5} = \frac{\square}{10}$ b) $\frac{3}{9} = \frac{1}{\square}$ c) $\frac{6}{8} = \frac{3}{\square}$

From: **Fractions 4 Teacher's Guide** © Schofield & Sims Ltd, 2017. This page may be photocopied after purchase.

→ Starting point

Show the number line and the first question in the **Starting point** graphic. Ask:
- *What is $\frac{3}{10}$ plus $\frac{6}{10}$? How can we find out?* Discuss different ways to use the number line; for example, count on $\frac{6}{10}$ from $\frac{3}{10}$ or count on $\frac{3}{10}$ from $\frac{6}{10}$. [Both methods give the answer $\frac{9}{10}$.]
- *What do you notice about the numerator of the answer?* [It is the total of the two numerators in the question.]
- *What do you notice about the denominator of the answer?* [It is the same as those in the question and has not changed.]

Show the subtraction question. Ask:
- *What if we are subtracting? What is $\frac{9}{10}$ take away $\frac{2}{10}$?* [$\frac{7}{10}$] Draw attention again to the fact that the denominator of the answer is the same as the denominators in the question.

Show the third question. Ask:
- *What is the sum of $\frac{3}{10}$ and $\frac{8}{10}$?* Use the number line to show this addition by counting on.
- *How can we write this answer?* [$\frac{11}{10}$ or $1\frac{1}{10}$] Explain that the numerators can be added together to give 11 and the answer is $\frac{11}{10}$ (an improper or top heavy fraction). The answer can also be given as the mixed number $1\frac{1}{10}$.

Show the last question. Ask:
- *Can you give the answer to this last question first as an improper fraction and then as a mixed number?* [$\frac{17}{10}$, $1\frac{7}{10}$]

> **Key point:** For fractions with the same denominator, only the numerators are added or subtracted. The denominator of the answer is the same.

○ Spot the mistake

Ask:
- *The statement says '$\frac{4}{5} + \frac{4}{5} = \frac{8}{10}$'. Is this true?* [no] *What is the mistake?* [The denominators have been added as well as the numerators, which is incorrect.]
- *What should the answer be as an improper fraction?* [$\frac{8}{5}$]
- *What should the answer be as a mixed number?* [$1\frac{3}{5}$]

✓ Good to go?

Answers: a) $\frac{2}{7}$ **b)** $\frac{7}{8}$ **c)** $\frac{5}{4}$ or $1\frac{1}{4}$

> ### Pupil book practice
> **Pages 14 and 15**
>
> Ensure that the pupils know the words 'improper fraction', 'difference' and 'decrease'. For question 16 they should also be able to select the largest and smallest fraction from a group of fractions with the same denominator. The **Challenge** questions include some equivalence work where the pupils can use the fact that $\frac{5}{15}$ is equivalent to $\frac{1}{3}$ to begin to add fractions with different denominators. They will also need to know or be able to work out that $\frac{1}{12}$ of an hour is 5 minutes for the final question. It may help to demonstrate this using a clock in the classroom.

Starting point

0 — 1 — 2

$\frac{3}{10} + \frac{6}{10} = \frac{\square}{\square}$

$\frac{9}{10} - \frac{2}{10} = \frac{\square}{\square}$

$\frac{3}{10} + \frac{8}{10} = \frac{\square}{\square}$ or $\square$

$\frac{8}{10} + \frac{9}{10} = \frac{\square}{\square}$ or $\square$

Spot the mistake

$\frac{4}{5} + \frac{4}{5} = \frac{8}{10}$

Good to go?

a) $\frac{6}{7} - \frac{4}{7} = \frac{\square}{\square}$

b) $\frac{3}{8} + \frac{4}{8} = \frac{\square}{\square}$

c) $\frac{3}{4} + \frac{2}{4} = \frac{\square}{\square}$ or $\square$

From: **Fractions 4 Teacher's Guide** © Schofield & Sims Ltd, 2017. This page may be photocopied after purchase.

Starting point

Show the first circle in graphic **A** and explain that it is split into tenths. Ask:

- *What fraction of the circle is shaded?* [$\frac{1}{10}$] Explain that the proportion that is shaded can also be described as 'a decimal'.

Reveal the next two columns for the first circle to show $\frac{1}{10}$ and 0.1. Ask:

- *Does anyone know what this dot is called?* [a decimal point] Establish that the column to the right of the decimal point shows how many tenths there are. Explain that $\frac{1}{10}$ can also be shown as 0.1.

Show the second and third rows.

- *What fraction of the second circle is shaded?* [$\frac{2}{10}$] *How do we write this as a decimal?* [0.2]
- *What fraction of the third circle is shaded?* [$\frac{5}{10}$] *How do we write this as a decimal?* [0.5]
- *Which decimal is the same as $\frac{1}{2}$?* Encourage the pupils to see that $\frac{5}{10}$ is equal to 0.5 and that $\frac{5}{10}$ is equivalent to $\frac{1}{2}$.

Reveal the last row. Ask:

- *How could we write what fraction of these circles are shaded as a mixed number?* [$1\frac{4}{10}$]
- *How do you think we would write this as a decimal?* [1.4] Explain that the 1 stands for 1 whole or 1 one (in the ones column) and so comes before the decimal point. The 4 stands for 4 tenths and this goes in the column to the right of the decimal point.

Show graphic **B** and discuss the answers. [$\frac{7}{10}$, 2.9]

> **Key point:** The column to the right of a decimal point is the tenths column. Decimals with a digit after the decimal point show how many wholes and how many tenths there are.

Spot the mistake

Ask:

- The statement says '3.2kg is $\frac{3}{10}$ of a kilogram more than 2 whole kilograms'. Is this true? [no]
- *Why isn't it true?* [2 whole kilograms should be written with a 2 before the decimal point and $\frac{3}{10}$ of a kilogram should be written with a 3 in the tenths column (after the decimal point).]
- *What is the correct answer?* [2.3kg is $\frac{3}{10}$ of a kilogram more than 2 whole kilograms *or* 3.2kg is $\frac{2}{10}$ of a kilogram more than 3 whole kilograms.]

Good to go?

Answers: a) 0.3   **b)** 0.9   **c)** 0.6   **d)** 3.8   **e)** 0.5   **f)** 6.1

> ### Pupil book practice   Pages 18 and 19
>
> In **Fractions 3** the pupils became familiar with tenths in relation to fractions. These questions consolidate this learning and extend it to include the decimal notation for tenths. The pupils may need to be reminded that, when a number is divided by 10, the result will be that number of tenths, for example, $4 \div 10 = \frac{4}{10}$. The **Now try these** and **Challenge** sections include some equivalence, encouraging the pupils to understand that $\frac{5}{10}$ or 0.5 is equivalent to $\frac{1}{2}$.

Starting point

A	tenths	fraction/mixed number	decimal ones . tenths
	(1/10 shaded circle)	$\frac{1}{10}$	0 . 1
	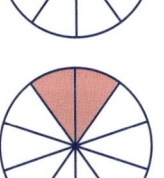	$\frac{\square}{10}$	0 . $\square$
	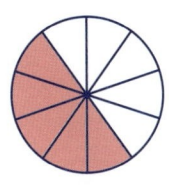	$\frac{\square}{10}$	0 . $\square$
	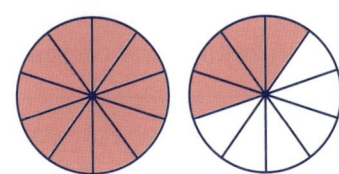	$1\frac{\square}{10}$	1 . $\square$

B How do you write: 0.7 as a fraction?

$2\frac{9}{10}$ as a decimal?

Spot the mistake

3.2 kg is $\frac{3}{10}$ of a kilogram more than 2 whole kilograms.

Good to go?

Write each as a decimal.

a) 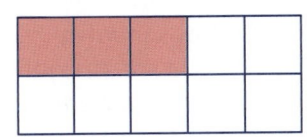 b) $\frac{9}{10}$ c) six-tenths

d) $3\frac{8}{10}$ e) $\frac{1}{2}$ f) 6 ones and 1 tenth

From: **Fractions 4 Teacher's Guide** © Schofield & Sims Ltd, 2017. This page may be photocopied after purchase.

→ Starting point

Display the number line in graphic **A**. Remind the pupils that fractions and decimals are two different ways of describing the same thing. Ask:

- *How do you say these fractions aloud?* [one-tenth, two-tenths, etc.] Count forwards along the line to 1 whole and remind the pupils that $\frac{10}{10}$ is 1 whole. Continue counting with mixed numbers [one and one-tenth, one and two-tenths, etc.] beyond those marked on the number line.
- *How do you say these decimals aloud?* [zero point one, zero point two, etc.] Count forwards along the line to 1 and remind the pupils that 1.0 is the same as 1 because both mean 1 whole and no tenths. Again continue counting beyond those decimals marked on the number line.
- *Which decimal is the same as $\frac{1}{2}$?* [0.5]
- *Why is 0.5 the same as $\frac{1}{2}$?* Encourage the pupils to see that $\frac{5}{10}$ is equal to 0.5 and that $\frac{5}{10}$ is equivalent to $\frac{1}{2}$.

Reveal the two questions in graphic **B**. Ask:

- *What decimal would the mark between 1.6 and 1.8 stand for?* [1.7]
- *How could you describe this as a mixed number?* [$1\frac{7}{10}$]
- *What decimal would the mark between 3.9 and 4.1 stand for?* [4 or 4.0] Again remind the pupils that 4 and 4.0 have the same value as they both mean 4 wholes and no tenths.

> **Key point:** Tenths less than one whole can be described as fractions or as decimals with one digit after the decimal point, where this digit is the tenths digit. Tenths greater than one whole can be described as mixed numbers, improper fractions or decimals.

🔍 Spot the mistake

Ask:

- *Look at this number line. Is the arrow labelled correctly?* [no]
- *What is wrong with the label for the arrow?* [It is showing the wrong decimal.]
- *How do you know?* [The decimal shows no wholes but the mark lies between the whole numbers 6 and 7 and so should have 6 wholes.]
- *What is the correct label for this arrow?* [6.7]

✓ Good to go?

Answers: a) $1\frac{2}{10}$ b) 3.8   c) 5.1   d) 4.2

> **Pupil book practice**   Pages 20 and 21
>
> These questions provide opportunities for the pupils to use tenths as decimals related to measures including millimetres, centimetres, metres, kilograms and litres. There is also some further practice of the equivalence of 0.5 and $\frac{1}{2}$. Many of the questions involve continuing sequences or comparing decimals on a number line. If any pupils are struggling, give them number lines showing tenths written as decimals (available to download from the Schofield & Sims website) so that they can use them to count forwards and backwards.

Starting point

A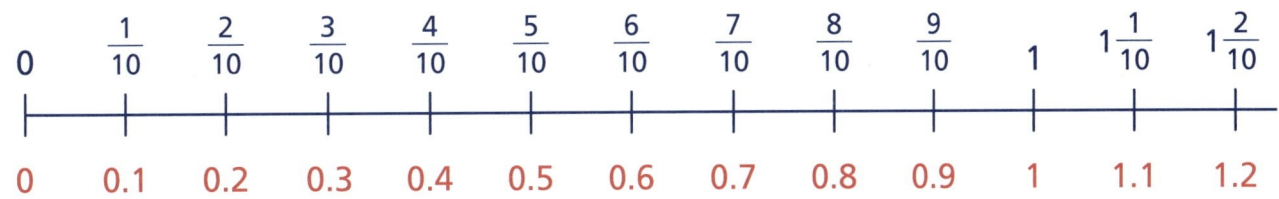

B If the line were extended, what decimal would be between:

1.6 and 1.8?

3.9 and 4.1?

Spot the mistake

Good to go?

Which numbers are missing?

a) $\frac{9}{10}$, 1, $1\frac{1}{10}$, ___ , $1\frac{3}{10}$

b) 3.5, 3.6, 3.7, ___ , 3.9

c) 4.8, 4.9, 5, ___ , 5.2

d) 4.3, ___ , 4.1, 4, 3.9

From: **Fractions 4 Teacher's Guide** © Schofield & Sims Ltd, 2017. This page may be photocopied after purchase.

Starting point

Display graphic **A**. Ask:

- *How long is the top line? Can you give your answer as a fraction and as a decimal?* [$\frac{9}{10}$ cm, 0.9cm]
- *How long is the bottom line as a fraction and as a decimal?* [$2\frac{3}{10}$ cm, 2.3cm]

Show graphic **B**. Discuss which is larger and how to show this using the greater than or less than signs (< or >). [0.9 < 2.3]

Now reveal graphic **C** and ask:

- *If you had to give each of these decimals as a whole number, which numbers would you use?* Explain that this is called rounding to the nearest whole number. Demonstrate that 0.9 is rounded to 1 and 2.3 is rounded to 2.
- *What is 1.5 rounded to the nearest whole number? Which whole number is it closest to?* Find 1.5 on the ruler and point out that it is exactly halfway between 1 and 2. Explain that, in this case, the number is rounded up to the higher of the two numbers. [2]
- *What is 7.2 to the nearest whole number?* [7]

> **Key point:** When rounding to the nearest whole number, find which number the decimal is closest to. If it is halfway between two whole numbers (for example, if the tenths digit is 5), then round up.

Spot the mistake

Ask:

- *When rounding to the nearest whole number, does 3.5 round to 3?* [no]
- *Why not?* [It ends in 5 tenths, so it is rounded up to the next whole number.]
- *What is the correct answer?* [4]

Good to go?

Answers: a) 0.1, 0.3, 0.4, 0.6   **b)** 1.0, 1.3, 1.4, 1.9   **c)** 0.6, 1.5, 1.8, 2.0   **d)** 6.1, 6.7, 7.0, 7.6

> ## Pupil book practice
> **Pages 22 and 23**
>
> The questions provide a wide range of practice in comparing, ordering and rounding decimals involving tenths, while making frequent links to their relationship with fractions and mixed numbers. Some problems involve measurements including centimetres, metres, kilograms and units of time. The pupils will need to have an appreciation of a whole being worth $\frac{10}{10}$ and thus be able to work out how many tenths are in 1.3 in total ($\frac{10}{10}$ forming the whole and $\frac{3}{10}$ makes 13 tenths).

Starting point

A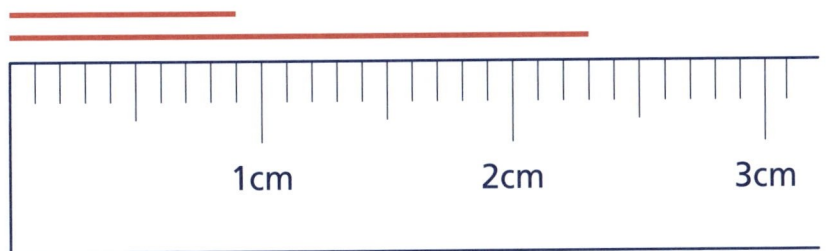

B Show which is larger using the < or > sign.

   0.9  2.3

C Round each decimal to the nearest whole number.
   0.9   2.3   1.5   7.2

Spot the mistake

When rounded to the nearest whole number, 3.5 rounds to 3.

Good to go?

Put these decimals in order from smallest to largest.

a) 0.6, 0.3, 0.1, 0.4

b) 1.4, 1.9, 1.3, 1.0

c) 1.5, 2.0, 0.6, 1.8

d) 7.6, 6.7, 6.1, 7.0

➔ Starting point

Display the first division question and the first circle in graphic **A**. Ask:

- *Imagine there are 10 people and I am sharing a pie between them. What is 1 pie shared equally between 10?* [Each person has $\frac{1}{10}$ which is 0.1.]

Show the second division question and related circles. Ask:

- *What if I had 2 pies to share between the 10 people? How much would they each get? How could I find out?* Discuss how one way would be to cut both pies into 10 slices and give everyone a slice from both pies. [Each person gets $\frac{2}{10}$ which is 0.2.]

Show the third division question and related circles. Ask:

- *So what do you think the answer to 3 divided by 10 is? How much would each of the 10 people get if 3 pies were shared?* Remind the pupils that all 3 pies could be cut into 10 slices and each person could have a slice from each. [Each person gets $\frac{3}{10}$ which is 0.3.]

Now display the place value grid in graphic **B**. Ask:

- *Can you tell me what happens to the digits of the number when you divide by 10? What do you notice about the digits in the question and answer?* [The digit moves one place to the right.]

> **Key point:** Tenths are often created when whole numbers are divided by 10. The digit or digits of the number being divided by 10 move one place to the right.

🔍 Spot the mistake

Ask:

- *The statement says '9 ÷ 10 = 9.0'. Is this true?* [no]
- *What mistake has been made?* [The digit 9 has not been moved one place to the right.]
- *What is the correct answer?* [0.9]

✓ Good to go?

Answers: a) 0.8   **b)** 4   **c)** 0.9m

The pupils might give the answer 4.0 for **b)**, which is also correct.

> ### Pupil book practice   Pages 24 and 25
> The questions provide practice in dividing by 10 to give answers in words and using correct notation as both fractions and decimals. They mainly use measurement contexts where quantities or lengths are divided into 10 or equally shared between 10. Problems also involve the inverse of dividing by 10, such as finding the length of 10 lots of 0.6m. Note that question 21 requires an understanding of the equivalence of $\frac{5}{10}$ and $\frac{1}{2}$ while question 22 introduces $\frac{1}{5}$ as being equivalent to $\frac{2}{10}$ and therefore being the decimal 0.2. The following unit continues these ideas and extends them to two-digit numbers.

Starting point

A

1 ÷ 10 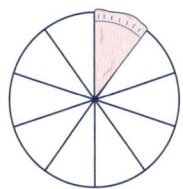 = $\frac{1}{10}$ = 0.1

2 ÷ 10 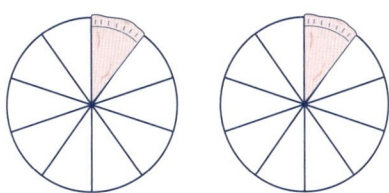 = $\frac{2}{10}$ = 0.2

3 ÷ 10 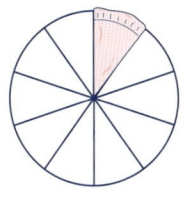 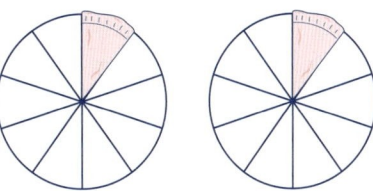 = $\frac{3}{10}$ = 0.3

B

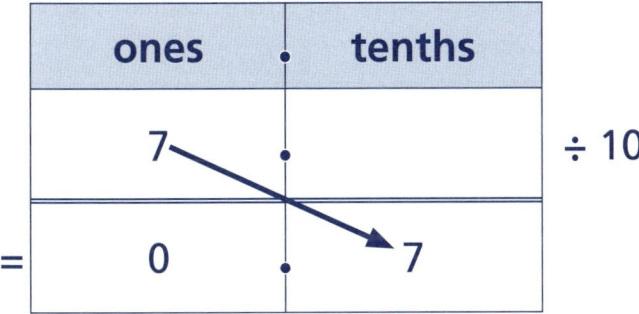

Spot the mistake

9 ÷ 10 = 9.0

Good to go?

Answer these. Give your answer as a decimal.

a) 8 ÷ 10 =

b) ☐ ÷ 10 = 0.4

c) 9m of ribbon is cut into 10 equal parts. How long is each part as a decimal?

➡️ Starting point

Show the first question in the **Starting point** graphic, without the place value grid. Ask:

- *If I had 13 cakes and shared them between 10 people, how much would they each get? How could we work this out?* Encourage the pupils to imagine this situation and remind them that, if there were 10 cakes to share between 10, the question would be easier. Establish that 1 cake could be given to each person and then the 3 remaining cakes shared out so that each person has an extra $\frac{3}{10}$ of cake. This would make the answer 1 whole and 3 tenths.

Now ask:

- *How do we write this answer as a decimal?* [1.3] Remind the pupils that there is a quick way to divide by 10 – move the digits one place to the right. Reveal the place value grid to show this.

Reveal the next question. Ask:

- *What is 54 divided by 10?* [5.4] Demonstrate moving the digits.

Reveal the next question. Ask:

- *What is 70 divided by 10?* [7 or 7.0] Demonstrate moving the digits. Emphasise that 7.0 and 7 have the same value because both stand for 7 wholes and no tenths. Explain that 'point zero' is not needed here.

> **Key point:** When dividing any number by 10, the digits of the number move one place to the right. If the number being divided by 10 is a multiple of 10, it is not necessary to write the zero at the end.

🔍 Spot the mistake

Ask:

- *The statement says '39 × 10 = 3.9'. Is this true?* [no]
- *What is the mistake?* [The statement has a multiplication sign rather than a division sign.]
- *How can we change the statement to make it true?* [Either replace × with ÷ or swap the numbers round to read 3.9 × 10 = 39]

✔️ Good to go?

Answers: a) 2.8   **b)** 4.7   **c)** 32   **d)** 7.3   **e)** 60   **f)** 9

The pupils might give the answer 9.0 for **f)**, which is also correct.

> ### Pupil book practice
> **Pages 26 and 27**
>
> This concept is one that the pupils will master competently with sufficient practice. The questions provide varied practice in many different contexts including measurement and money problems. These include beginning to divide whole lengths by 10 to give decimal answers, for example, 5.2cm. Question 19 tests understanding of the equivalence of 0.5 and $\frac{1}{2}$. Question 24 involves writing $\frac{9}{10}$ of £6 as a decimal. Encourage the pupils to see that £5.4 is not usually how money is written and that £5.40 means the same amount but is written in a better way.

Starting point

13 ÷ 10 = ☐

tens	ones	.	tenths	
1	3	.		÷ 10
	1	.	3	

=

54 ÷ 10 = ☐

70 ÷ 10 = ☐

Spot the mistake

39 × 10 = 3.9

Good to go?

a) 28 ÷ 10 = ☐

b) 47 ÷ 10 = ☐

c) ☐ ÷ 10 = 3.2

d) 73 ÷ 10 = ☐

e) ☐ ÷ 10 = 6

f) 90 ÷ 10 = ☐

➡ Starting point

Show the first question and circles in graphic **A** but not the answer. Ask:
- *How can we find the answer to 3 cakes divided by 8?* [Split each cake into eighths and give each person $\frac{1}{8}$ from each cake.] Reveal the answer $\frac{3}{8}$.
- *What do you notice about the numbers in the question and answer?* [They are the same.]

To test if this always works, show the next question and its related circles. Ask:
- *What is 4 cakes shared between 5?* [Each cake is split into fifths and each person has a fifth from each cake giving the answer $\frac{4}{5}$.] Reveal the answer.
- *What do you notice about the numbers in the question and answer?* [They are the same.]

Repeat for $3 \div 10$ in the same way, also showing the answer as a decimal.

Display graphic **B**. Ask:
- *Can you describe the method for writing the answer to a division question as a fraction?* [The number being divided is the numerator and the number you are dividing by is the denominator.]

> **Key point:** When dividing, the number being divided becomes the numerator and the number being divided by (the divisor) becomes the denominator.

🔍 Spot the mistake

Ask:
- *The statement says that '$4 \div 7 = \frac{7}{4}$'. Is this true?* [no]
- *What is the mistake?* [The numerator and denominator are the wrong way round.]
- *So what is the correct answer?* [$\frac{4}{7}$]

✓ Good to go?

Answers: a) $\frac{5}{9}$ b) $\frac{11}{12}$ c) $\frac{6}{7}$ d) $\frac{8}{10}$

The pupils might give the answer $\frac{4}{5}$ for **d)**, which is also correct.

> ## Pupil book practice   Pages 28 and 29
>
> In the **Now try these** and **Challenge** sections, the pupils are expected to use equivalence to begin to write fractions in a simpler form, for example, $6 \div 8 = \frac{\blacksquare}{\blacksquare} = \frac{\blacksquare}{4}$, and to understand that $\frac{1}{2}$ is a better answer than $\frac{4}{8}$. The last two questions involve dividing a larger number by a smaller one to give either an improper fraction, a mixed number or a decimal.

Starting point

A

$3 \div 8 =$ 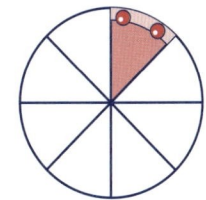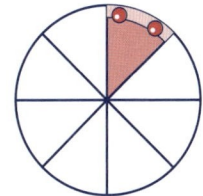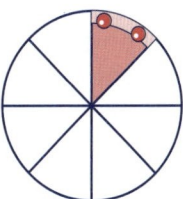 $\frac{3}{8}$

$4 \div 5 =$ 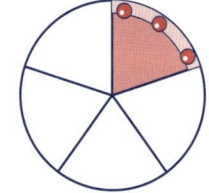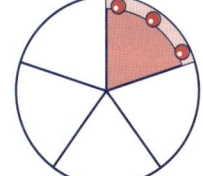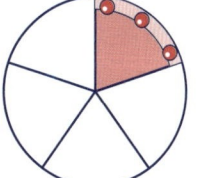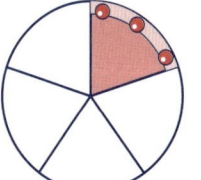 $\frac{4}{5}$

$3 \div 10 =$ 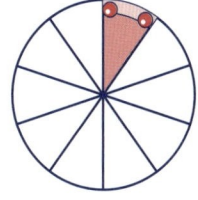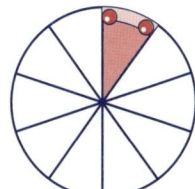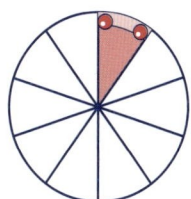 $\frac{3}{10}$ or 0.3

B

$7 \div 8 = \frac{7}{8}$

Spot the mistake

$4 \div 7 = \frac{7}{4}$

Good to go?

a) $5 \div 9 = \dfrac{}{}$

b) $11 \div 12 = \dfrac{}{}$

c) $6 \div 7 = \dfrac{}{}$

d) $8 \div 10 = \dfrac{}{}$

Starting point

Show the squares in graphic **A**. Point out that the first square is split into tenths and the next two are split into hundredths. Ask:

- *What fraction of the first square is shaded?* [$\frac{1}{10}$] Reiterate that 1 tenth can be written both as a fraction and as a decimal (where the column to the right of the decimal point shows the number of tenths). Reveal the fraction [$\frac{1}{10}$] and the decimal [0.1].
- *What fraction of the second square is shaded?* [$\frac{1}{100}$]
- *Do you know how to write this as a decimal?* [0.01] Explain that the column to the right of the tenths shows how many hundredths there are.

Look at the third square, show the fraction and challenge the pupils to guess how this is written as a decimal. [0.14] Ask:

- *Why is there a 1 in the tenths column?* [10 of the hundredths make up 1 tenth.] Help the pupils to see that 14 hundredths is the same as 1 tenth and 4 hundredths, so the decimal is 0.14.

Display the squares in graphic **B**. Ask:

- *What fraction of the first square is shaded?* [$\frac{1}{4}$] *How many is $\frac{1}{4}$ of 100?* [25]
- *So how many hundredths do you think is $\frac{1}{4}$?* [25 hundredths]. *How then do you think that we write $\frac{1}{4}$ (25 hundredths) as a decimal?* [0.25].

Repeat for $\frac{3}{4}$ [0.75] and $\frac{1}{2}$ [0.5].

> **Key point:** The column to the right of the tenths column is the hundredths column. 10 hundredths is equal to 1 tenth so, if there are more than 9 hundredths, use the tenths column. For example, 12 hundredths is written as 0.12.

Spot the mistake

Ask:

- *The statement says '$\frac{6}{100}$ kg = 0.6kg'. Is this true?* [no]
- *What is the mistake?* [0.6 means 6 tenths, not 6 hundredths.]
- *How could we change this statement to make it true?* [Either change the fraction to $\frac{6}{10}$ or change the decimal to 0.06.]

Good to go?

Answers: a) 0.02   b) 0.09   c) 0.06   d) 0.83   e) 0.75   f) 0.14

> # Pupil book practice
> **Pages 32 and 33**
>
> In Unit 7 of this book the pupils learnt about tenths in relation to fractions and decimals. If you find any pupils struggling with hundredths, you may like to encourage them to redo Unit 7 to consolidate those ideas first. It is important that the pupils are confident with fraction notation for this unit. The **Challenge** section includes application of hundredths to measurement problems and begins to make the link between centimetres and metres where 1cm = $\frac{1}{100}$ of a metre = 0.01m. Practical equipment such as a metre ruler or tape measures can be used to demonstrate this link if required.

Starting point

		fraction	decimal ones . tenths hundredths
A 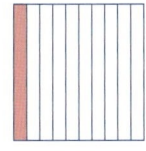	1 tenth	$\frac{1}{10}$	0 . 1
	1 hundredth	$\frac{1}{100}$	0 . 0 1
	14 hundredths	$\frac{14}{100}$	0 . 1 4
B 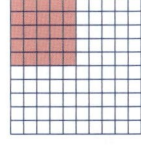	1 quarter	$\frac{1}{4}$ or $\frac{25}{100}$	0 . 2 5
	3 quarters	$\frac{3}{4}$ or $\frac{75}{100}$	0 . 7 5
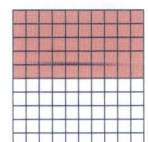	1 half	$\frac{1}{2}$ or $\frac{50}{100}$	0 . 5 0

Spot the mistake

$\frac{6}{100}$ kg = 0.6kg

Good to go?

Write each as a decimal.

a) 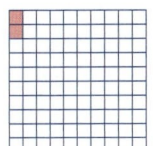   b) $\frac{9}{100}$ c) 6 hundredths

d) $\frac{83}{100}$ e) $\frac{3}{4}$ f) 1 tenth and 4 hundredths

From: **Fractions 4 Teacher's Guide** © *Schofield & Sims Ltd, 2017. This page may be photocopied after purchase.*

Starting point

Display graphic **A**. Begin by revising counting on in tenths. Ask:

- *What is 1 tenth more than 3 tenths?* [$\frac{4}{10}$ or 0.4] Count on in tenths as fractions and as decimals and make the link between this and the squares above that show tenths.

Point out the little marks between 0 and 0.1. Ask:

- *Do you think we can describe points on the line between the main marks? Can you think of anything smaller than a tenth?* Guide the pupils towards the answer 'hundredths'. Point out that the little marks represent hundredths.

Reveal graphic **B**. Point out that it is a close up of a section of number line **A**, between 0 and 0.1 where the little marks are. Ask:

- *Can you see that 1 hundredth is smaller than 1 tenth? Can you count in hundredths from zero to 1 tenth?* Point out that 10 hundredths are the same as 1 tenth. Count as both fractions and as decimals. Then begin to count on along the line beyond 0.1.
- *What numbers come between 1 tenth and 2 tenths?* [11 hundredths (0.11), 12 hundredths (0.12), 13 hundredths (0.13), and so on]

Encourage the pupils to count on in decimals between other pairs of tenths and to recognise that between 0.5 and 0.6, for example, decimals will start with 0.5, as in, 0.51, 0.52, and so on.

> **Key point:** Hundredths can describe points between tenths on a number line. Between 0 and 0.1 are 0.01, 0.02, 0.03 and so on. Between 0.1 and 0.2 decimals start with 0.1. Between 0.2 and 0.3 decimals start with 0.2, and so on.

Spot the mistake

Ask:

- Look at this number line. Is the arrow labelled correctly? [no]
- What is wrong with the label for the arrow? [It is showing the wrong decimal.]
- How do you know? [It should show 3 tenths and 7 hundredths.]
- What is the correct label for this arrow? [0.37]

Good to go?

Answers: a) $\frac{9}{100}$ **b)** 0.07   **c)** 0.49   **d)** 0.6

The pupils might give the answer 0.60 for **d)**, which is also correct.

> ## Pupil book practice   Pages 34 and 35
>
> The questions provide opportunities for the pupils to practise hundredths shown as fractions, decimals and in words and to identify them on number lines. They also begin to relate decimals to measures including centimetres, metres and litres. If any pupils are struggling, give them number lines showing hundredths written as decimals (available to download from the Schofield & Sims website) to use to count forwards and backwards.

Starting point

A

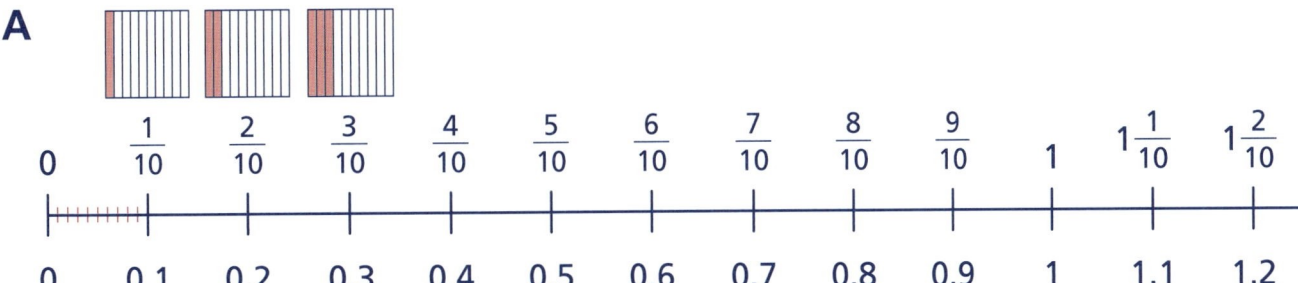

B

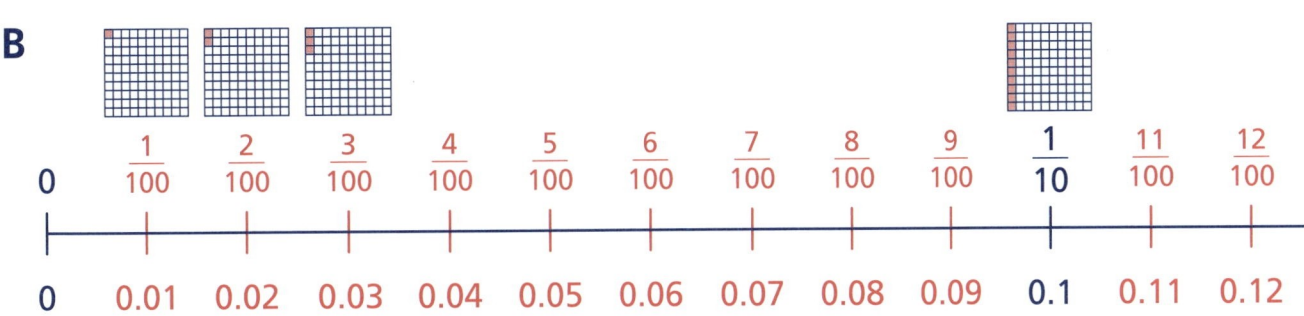

Spot the mistake

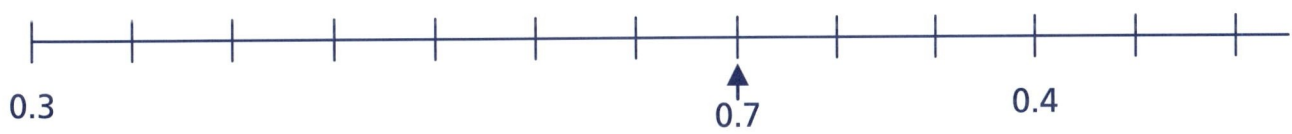

Good to go?

What numbers are missing?

a) $\frac{7}{100}$, $\frac{8}{100}$, ___, $\frac{1}{10}$, $\frac{11}{100}$

b) 0.04, 0.05, 0.06, ___

c) 0.46, 0.47, 0.48, ___

d) 0.58, 0.59, ___, 0.61

From: **Fractions 4 Teacher's Guide** © Schofield & Sims Ltd, 2017. This page may be photocopied after purchase.

Starting point

Show the first two rows in graphic **A** to revise describing hundredths as both fractions and decimals. Ask:

- *How many more hundredths would we need to colour in so that the whole square is shaded?* [98 hundredths for first square and 86 hundredths for the second square]

Now reveal the two squares in the final row of graphic **A**, but keep the notation hidden. Ask:

- *How many hundredths are shaded in these two squares altogether?* [100 + 13 = 113 hundredths or $\frac{113}{100}$]
- *How do we write this as a decimal?* [1.13] Explain that, since 100 hundredths is 1 whole or 1 one, they should put a 1 in the ones column. Since 10 hundredths is 1 tenth they should put a 1 in the tenths column and the 3 hundredths in the hundredths column, giving the answer 1.13. Reveal the notation.

Display graphic **B** and ask:

- *Which sign should we put between 0.53 and 0.49?* [>]
- *What about between 1.24 and 0.95?* [>] Discuss ways of deciding which is larger, describing each number in relation to wholes, tenths and hundredths.

> **Key point:** 100 hundredths is 1 whole (1 one). 10 hundredths is 1 tenth. When comparing decimals, think first which has more ones, then which has more tenths and then which has more hundredths.

Spot the mistake

Ask:

- *Is 0.50 smaller than 0.05?* [no]
- *What do these decimals stand for?* [0.50 is 50 hundredths or 5 tenths and 0.05 stands for 5 hundredths.]
- *Which is larger, 1 tenth or 1 hundredth?* [1 tenth]
- *So which decimal is larger?* [0.50]
- *Which sign should the statement use?* [>]

Good to go?

Answers: a) 0.03, 0.15, 0.53   b) 0.04, 0.10, 0.18   c) 1.36, 1.47, 2.05   d) 5.07, 5.10, 5.63

> ## Pupil book practice   Pages 36 and 37
>
> The pupil book provides a wide range of practice in comparing and ordering decimals involving hundredths, and makes frequent links to their relationship with fractions and mixed numbers. Problems involve measurements including centimetres, metres, kilograms and money. The pupils will need to have an appreciation of a whole being equivalent to 100 hundredths and 10 hundredths being equivalent to 1 tenth.

→ Starting point

A   fraction   decimal
 ones . tenths hundredths

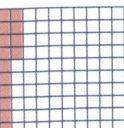   2 hundredths $\frac{2}{100}$ 0 . 0 2

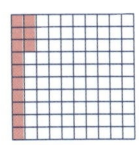   14 hundredths $\frac{14}{100}$ 0 . 1 4

   113 hundredths $\frac{113}{100}$ 1 . 1 3

B Show which is larger using the < or > sign.

0.53 ☐ 0.49   1.24 ☐ 0.95

🔍 Spot the mistake

0.50 < 0.05

✓ Good to go?

Put these decimals in order from smallest to largest.

a) 0.53, 0.15, 0.03

b) 0.04, 0.18, 0.10

c) 1.47, 1.36, 2.05

d) 5.10, 5.07, 5.63

From: **Fractions 4 Teacher's Guide** © Schofield & Sims Ltd, 2017. This page may be photocopied after purchase.

Divide one- or two-digit numbers by 100

→ Starting point

Show the first question in the **Starting point** graphic, without the place value grid. Ask:

- *If I had £37 and shared it equally between 100 people, how much would they each get? How could we work this out?* Encourage the pupils to consider whether each person would get more or less than £1. Remind the pupils that when dividing by 10, the digits of the number can be moved one place to the right. In this instance this would give the answer 3.7 or £3.70.
- *So, what do you think we might do to divide by 100?* [Move the digits two places to the right.] Reveal the place value grid to demonstrate how the answer £0.37 or 37p can be found.

Display the next question. Ask:

- *What is 54 divided by 100?* [0.54] Demonstrate moving the digits.

Display the next question. Ask:

- *What is 70 divided by 100?* [0.70 or 0.7] Demonstrate moving the digits. Show the pupils that 0.70 and 0.7 have the same value because both stand for 7 tenths and no hundredths. Explain that the final zero is not needed after the decimal point.

> **Key point:** When dividing any number by 100, the digits of the number move two places to the right. If the number being divided by 100 is a multiple of 10 it is not necessary to write the zero at the end.

🔍 Spot the mistake

Ask:

- *The statement says '96 ÷ 100 = 9.6'. Is this true?* [no]
- *What is the mistake?* [The digits of 96 have only been moved one place to the right.]
- *How can we change the statement to make it true?* [Either make the answer 0.96 or change the question to 96 ÷ 10.]

✓ Good to go?

Answers: a) 0.28   **b)** 0.47   **c)** 72   **d)** 0.93   **e)** 60   **f)** 0.8

The pupils might give the answer 0.80 for **f)**, which is also correct.

> **Pupil book practice**   **Pages 38 and 39**
>
> Some pupils may benefit from being given a place value grid and cards to allow them to physically move the digits across two places. This concept is one that pupils master competently with sufficient practice. The questions provide varied practice in different contexts, including measurement and money problems. These include beginning to divide whole lengths by 100 to give decimal answers such as 0.04m. The **Challenge** questions involve some numbers with three digits where two are non-zero digits, for example, 130 or 707. Encourage the pupils to extend the place value grid to include hundreds and to move the digits across two places in the same way.

→ Starting point

37 ÷ 100 = ☐

tens	ones	.	tenths	hundredths	
3	7	.			÷ 100
	0	.	3	7	

=

54 ÷ 100 = ☐

70 ÷ 100 = ☐

🔍 Spot the mistake

96 ÷ 100 = 9.6

✓ Good to go?

a) 28 ÷ 100 = ☐

b) 47 ÷ 100 = ☐

c) ☐ ÷ 100 = 0.72

d) 93 ÷ 100 = ☐

e) ☐ ÷ 100 = 0.60

f) 80 ÷ 100 = ☐

Problems including finding fractions of amounts

→ Starting point

Show the first two rows in graphic **A**. Ask:
- *How can we find $\frac{1}{10}$ of £50?* [Divide £50 into 10 equal parts.]
- *Which number do we divide?* [the quantity, £50]
- *Which number do we divide by?* [the denominator (the bottom number), 10]
- *What is $\frac{1}{10}$ of £50?* [£5] Show the row of 10 lots of £5 making the total £50.

Now reveal the first row in graphic **B**. Ask:
- *How can we find $\frac{3}{10}$ of £50?* [Divide by 10 and then multiply by 3 to find $\frac{3}{10}$.]
- *What is $\frac{3}{10}$ of £50?* [£15] Reveal the row of 10 lots of £5 with three shaded.

Challenge the pupils to describe how to find a fraction of a number in their own words. Elicit the fact that you divide by the denominator and multiply by the numerator. Encourage the pupils to notice the first letters of the key words in this rule. Reveal graphic **C**. Ask:
- *How can we find $\frac{5}{6}$ of 24cm?* [Divide 24cm by 6 to find one-sixth and then multiply by 5 to find five-sixths.]
- *What is $\frac{5}{6}$ of 24cm?* [20cm]

> **Key point:** To find a fraction of a quantity, divide by the denominator (to find one part) and multiply by the numerator (to find the desired number of parts).

🔍 Spot the mistake

Ask:
- *The statement says '$\frac{3}{5}$ of 15 = 25'. Is this true?* [no]
- *What is the mistake?* [The quantity was divided by the numerator and multiplied by the denominator rather than the other way round.]
- *How can we make the statement true?* [$\frac{3}{5}$ of 15 = 15 ÷ 5 × 3 = 9]

✓ Good to go?

Answers: a) 18p **b)** £21 **c)** 14m

> ### Pupil book practice   Pages 40 and 41
> This practice focuses on finding fractions of numbers and measures. For those pupils who are not yet confident with their tables and division facts, this will be more challenging. You could provide them with a list of tables facts to refer to so that their focus can be on the process of finding fractions until they become confident. The **Challenge** questions require knowledge of the relationships between some of the units of measurement, such as 60 minutes equal 1 hour. In question 23, the pupils will also need to know how to find the perimeter of a rectangle.

Starting point

A

£50

$\frac{1}{10}$ of £50 = £50 ÷ 10 = £ ☐

| £5 | £5 | £5 | £5 | £5 | £5 | £5 | £5 | £5 | £5 |

B $\frac{3}{10}$ of £50 = £50 ÷ 10 × 3 = £ ☐

| £5 | £5 | £5 | £5 | £5 | £5 | £5 | £5 | £5 | £5 |

C **Divide** by the **denominator** (to find one part) and **multiply** by the **numerator** (to find several parts).

$\frac{\text{numerator}}{\text{denominator}}$ $\frac{5}{6}$ of 24cm = ☐ cm

Spot the mistake

$\frac{3}{5}$ of 15 = 25

Good to go?

a) Find $\frac{2}{3}$ of 27p.

b) Find $\frac{3}{4}$ of £28.

c) Find $\frac{7}{8}$ of 16m.

Starting point

Show graphic **A**. Remind the pupils that fractions can be used for measurements such as length, mass, capacity and amounts of money. Ask:

- *How many equal parts have these litre containers been split into?* [4] Discuss what fraction of a litre is shown in the first container [$\frac{3}{4}$l] and in the next two containers together. [$1\frac{3}{4}$l]

Show graphic **B**. Ask:

- *If these 5 weights make 1 kilogram, how many of these weights would be $\frac{2}{5}$ of a kilogram?* [2]

Show graphic **C**. Ask:

- *Each centimetre on this ruler is split into tenths. We can write the position of the arrow as a fraction and as a decimal. Can anyone explain what 0.9 means as a fraction and why?* [It means $\frac{9}{10}$ because when a number has a decimal point, the digit that follows it shows how many tenths there are.]

Show graphic **D**. Ask:

- *Each metre can be split into equal parts. How many equal parts has the first stick been split into?* [10] *What about the second stick?* [100]
- *Can anyone point to $\frac{7}{10}$ or 0.7 / $\frac{3}{100}$ or 0.03 / $\frac{99}{100}$ or 0.99 of a metre on these metre sticks?* Discuss each fraction and decimal pair in turn. Find each one on the metre sticks and discuss how they can each be a fraction or a decimal. Revise work done in previous units about how to show tenths and hundredths as decimals.

> **Key point:** Fractions and decimals can be used to show parts of a whole unit of measurement or money such as a kilogram, a metre, a litre, an hour or a pound.

Spot the mistake

Ask:

- *The statement says '$5\frac{1}{100}$kg = 5.1kg'. What is wrong with this?* [It incorrectly shows $5\frac{1}{100}$ as the decimal 5.1.]
- *How do we write 1 hundredth as a decimal?* [0.01]
- *What is 5 and 1 hundredth as a decimal?* [5.01]

Good to go?

Answers: a) 1p   **b)** 16cm   **c)** 5

> ### Pupil book practice   Pages 42 and 43
> These questions provide a variety of fraction, mixed number and decimal problems involving units of measurement and money. They include a range of question types from the whole programme and serve as revision of many of the ideas encountered. Some questions require an understanding of the link between fractional and decimal forms of the same number. The pupils will need to know the number of centimetres in a metre and the number of minutes in an hour. They must also understand how to find fractions of amounts and how to add and subtract them.

Fractions, Decimals and Percentages   Fractions 4 Teacher's Guide   Unit 18

 Starting point

A litres

B a kilogram

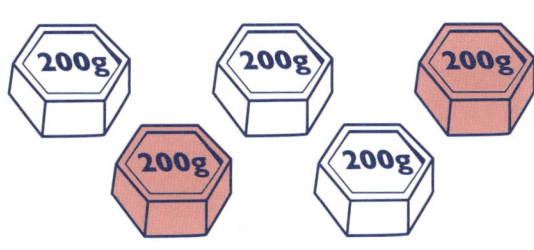

C centimetres

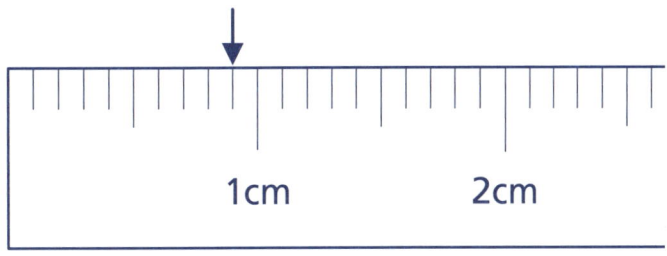

D metres

 Spot the mistake

$5\frac{1}{100}$ kg = 5.1 kg

 Good to go?

a) How many pence is £0.01?

b) How many centimetres is 0.16 m?

c) How many quarters of a kilogram are in $1\frac{1}{4}$ kg?

From: *Fractions 4 Teacher's Guide* © Schofield & Sims Ltd, 2017. This page may be photocopied after purchase.

ANSWERS UNIT 1

Understand the role of the numerator and denominator

Key point

The **denominator** shows how many equal parts the whole is split into.
The **numerator** shows how many of these parts are being described.

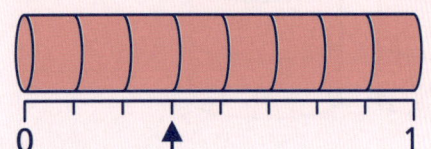

numerator ⟶ 3 The whole is split into **8 equal parts** and
denominator ⟶ 8 the fraction is showing **3 of those parts**.

Wholes can take many forms, including shapes, units of measurement, sets of objects, and numbers on a number line.

Get started

1 Colour $\frac{1}{8}$ of this circle.

2 What fraction of this rectangle is red?
$\frac{2}{3}$
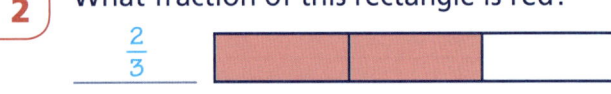

3 What is the denominator of three-quarters?
4

4 What is the numerator of three-fifths?
3

5 How many equal parts should this line be split into to show $\frac{1}{8}$?
8

6 True or false? The denominator of two-thirds is 2.
True ☐   False ✓

7 Colour one of these rectangles to show $\frac{2}{5}$.

8 A fraction has the denominator 5 and the numerator 4. Write this fraction in words.
four-fifths

Now try these

9 How many equal groups would you sort these flowers into to show $\frac{1}{6}$ of the whole set? ___6___

10 How many groups of flowers would be $\frac{5}{6}$ of the whole set? ___5___

11 What fraction does A stand for on the number line? $\frac{3}{5}$

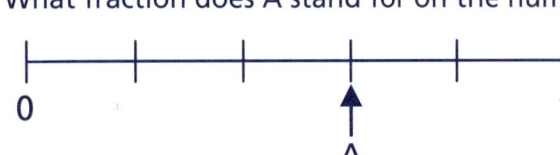

Fractions, Decimals and Percentages Fractions 4 Teacher's Guide Unit 1

12 Tick the diagram where $\frac{4}{7}$ of the shape is red.

☐   ✓   ☐

13 How many lots of $\frac{1}{10}$ are equal to $\frac{3}{10}$? ___3___

14 There are 3 yellow tennis balls and 5 green ones. What fraction of the balls are yellow? $\frac{3}{8}$

15 Jacob wants to colour some parts of this rectangle to show a fraction.
What will the denominator of the fraction be? ___5___

16 Anna says that three-fifths of this shape is red. Is she correct?

Yes ☐   No ✓

Challenge

17 The pupils in a class get into equal groups.
What fraction of the pupils in this class is 1 group? ___$\frac{1}{7}$___

18 How many pupils are there in $\frac{2}{7}$ of the class? ___4___

19 One-third of a 1kg bag of flour is put into a bowl.
What fraction of a kilogram is left in the bag? ___$\frac{2}{3}$___ kg

20 True or false? If the numerator of a fraction is larger than its denominator, the fraction is greater than one whole.   True ✓   False ☐

21 Abdul says that when the numerator of a fraction is the same as its denominator, the fraction is equivalent to the number 1. Is he correct?   Yes ✓   No ☐

22 A day has 24 hours. Bobby spent 7 hours asleep.
For what fraction of the day was he asleep? ___$\frac{7}{24}$___

23 Two fractions have the same numerator. Fraction A's denominator is larger than fraction B's denominator.
Circle the fraction that is larger.

fraction A   (fraction B)

24 Zainab writes a fraction with the numerator 1.
Her fraction is greater than one-third. What is the denominator of her fraction? ___2___

ANSWERS UNIT 2 — Schofield & Sims

Use fractions in different representations, including sets

Key point

Fractions can stand for areas of shapes, measurements, sets of objects, numbers on a line and so on.

To find fractions of sets of objects, **arrange them into equal groups**.

You can draw **loops** to divide these 18 squares into groups.

Each **row** is $\frac{1}{3}$.   Each **column** is $\frac{1}{6}$.

$\frac{2}{3}$ of 18 is **2** rows = 12 squares $\frac{5}{6}$ of 18 is **5** columns = 15 squares

Get started

1 Colour four-fifths of these fish.

2 How many squares in $\frac{1}{4}$ of this grid?   _6_

3 Mark $\frac{5}{8}$ on this line with a cross.

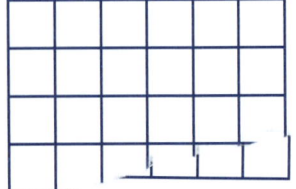
0   1

4 A loaf of bread is cut into seven equal slices. What fraction of the whole loaf is five slices? $\frac{5}{7}$

5 A bag of peppers contains 4 green and 5 red peppers. What fraction of the peppers are green? $\frac{4}{9}$

6 Colour seven-twelfths of this rectangle.

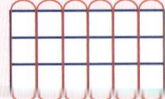

7 Write what fraction of the rectangle above is now not coloured. $\frac{5}{12}$

8 What fraction of the cubes are red? $\frac{2}{5}$ or $\frac{8}{20}$

Now try these

9 A packet contains 10 sweets. What fraction of the whole packet is 3 sweets? $\frac{3}{10}$

10 Colour $\frac{2}{3}$ of these caps.

Fractions, Decimals and Percentages

Fractions 4 Teacher's Guide Unit 2

11 What fraction of this rectangle is red? $\frac{3}{4}$
Write a fraction with the numerator 3.
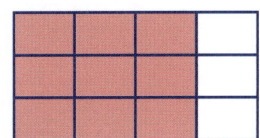

12 Colour four-fifths of this rectangle.

13 How many is $\frac{4}{5}$ of 10 squares? ___8___

14 How many pencils is five-sixths of a set of 18 pencils? ___15___

15 For each diagram, write the fraction of marbles that are white.
Give both fractions with the numerator 2.

a) 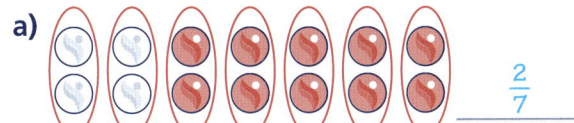 $\frac{2}{7}$

b) 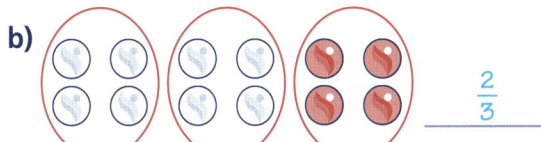 $\frac{2}{3}$

16 If A shows one-fifth of a litre, which letter shows $\frac{3}{5}$ of a litre? ___C___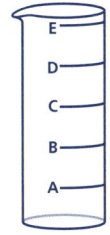

Challenge

17 On a battery the red part shows how much power remains. Estimate what fraction of the power remains. $\frac{1}{10}$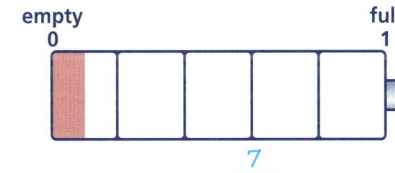

18 A centimetre is split into 10 millimetres. What fraction of a centimetre is 7mm? $\frac{7}{10}$ cm

19 Louise has five 20p coins, making a total of £1. What fraction of one pound is:
a) 20p? $\frac{1}{5}$ b) 60p? $\frac{3}{5}$

20 True or false? Three-quarters of 1 metre is 25cm. True ☐ False ✓

21 A box contains 4 red crayons, 2 yellow crayons and 5 blue crayons. What fraction of the crayons are:
a) red? $\frac{4}{11}$ b) yellow? $\frac{2}{11}$ c) blue? $\frac{5}{11}$

22 Of 12 mugs on the table, one-third are stripy. How many stripy mugs are there? ___4___

23 Tick more squares so that three-quarters of the squares in this grid are ticked.

24 A floor is made from 6 rows of 10 tiles all the same size. One-tenth of the tiles are coloured dark green and $\frac{1}{6}$ are light green. The rest are white. How many of the tiles are white? ___44___

ANSWERS UNIT 3

Recognise mixed numbers

Key point

Mixed numbers are numbers that include a whole number and a fraction, such as $4\frac{1}{2}$ or $5\frac{4}{5}$.

When finding mixed numbers on a number line, look carefully to see how many equal parts each whole number has been split into.

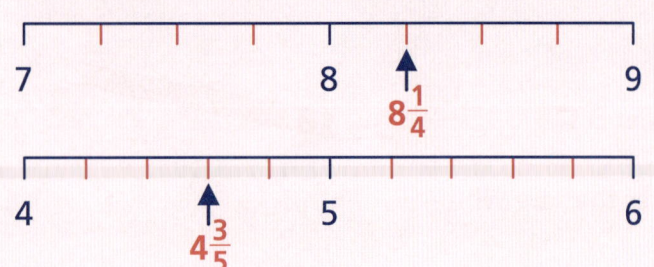

Here each whole is split into **quarters**.

Here each whole is split into **fifths**.

Get started

1 Write the number shown by the arrow. $3\frac{2}{3}$

2 Mark $2\frac{1}{3}$ on the line above with a cross.

3 What fraction is each part on this number line? $\frac{1}{8}$

4 What is three-eighths more than 5 wholes? $5\frac{3}{8}$

5 Which is larger: $4\frac{3}{5}$ or $5\frac{1}{3}$? $5\frac{1}{3}$

6 Write the next two numbers in this sequence.

4, $4\frac{1}{5}$, $4\frac{2}{5}$, $4\frac{3}{5}$, $4\frac{4}{5}$, __5__ , $5\frac{1}{5}$

7 Mark $\frac{5}{6}$ and $2\frac{3}{6}$ on this number line.

8 Circle the mixed number that lies between the whole numbers 2 and 3.

$1\frac{1}{3}$ $3\frac{1}{2}$ $1\frac{2}{3}$ ($2\frac{4}{5}$) $5\frac{2}{3}$ $3\frac{7}{8}$

Now try these

9 When writing the mixed number shown by the arrow, how many times will you write the digit 5? __2__

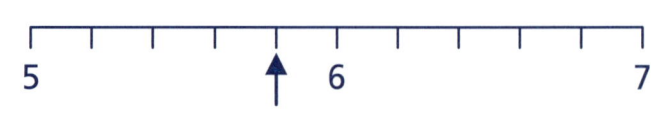

10 When counting on in sixths, which number comes next after $2\frac{5}{6}$? __3__

11 What is $\frac{4}{10}$ more than $3\frac{7}{10}$? $4\frac{1}{10}$

Fractions, Decimals and Percentages

Fractions 4 Teacher's Guide   Unit 3

12 Mark a cross on the ruler to show $2\frac{3}{10}$ cm.

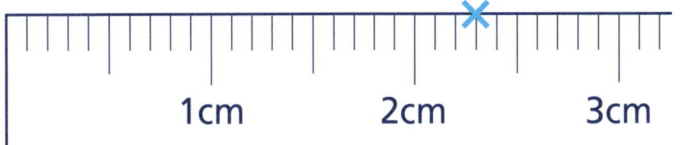

13 How many tenths in:

a) $\frac{7}{10}$? __7__   b) 3 wholes? __30__   c) $1\frac{5}{10}$? __15__

14 Isabel says that the mixed number $2\frac{5}{10}$ is halfway between 2 and 3. Is she correct?

Yes ✓   No ☐

15 Circle the fraction closest to the whole number 7.

$6\frac{1}{4}$ $7\frac{3}{4}$ $6\frac{1}{2}$ $7\frac{1}{2}$ $(6\frac{3}{4})$

16 True or false? $2\frac{2}{3}$ is greater than $3\frac{1}{3}$.   True ☐   False ✓

Challenge

17 Write these mixed numbers in order from smallest to largest.

$5\frac{2}{3}$ $1\frac{1}{3}$ $3\frac{1}{2}$ $2\frac{4}{5}$ __$1\frac{1}{3}$__   __$2\frac{4}{5}$__   __$3\frac{1}{2}$__   __$5\frac{2}{3}$__

18 Use the digits 7, 3 and 2 to write the smallest mixed number possible.   __$2\frac{3}{7}$__

19 Count on five-sixths from the arrow on the line. Which number do you land on?   __$7\frac{1}{6}$__

20 Jack jumps $4\frac{9}{10}$ m in the long jump. Caitlin jumps $5\frac{6}{10}$ m. How much further does Caitlin jump than Jack?   __$\frac{7}{10}$__ m

21 Count back three-eighths from 3. What mixed number do you reach?   __$2\frac{5}{8}$__

22 True or false? $1\frac{7}{12} + 7\frac{5}{12} = 9$ True ✓   False ☐

23 What mixed number is 6 less than $10\frac{7}{9}$?   __$4\frac{7}{9}$__

24 A builders' merchant sells bags of sand of different masses as shown here.
Chris buys 3 bags weighing a total of 20kg.
Which 3 bags does she buy? Circle them.

ANSWERS UNIT 4

Schofield & Sims

Find equivalent fractions using a fraction wall

Key point

Fractions that stand for the same amount are **equivalent**.

 $\frac{3}{4}$ is equivalent to $\frac{6}{8}$.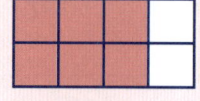

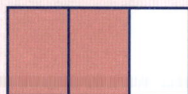 $\frac{2}{3}$ is equivalent to $\frac{6}{9}$.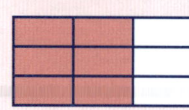

Use a **fraction wall** to find **equivalent fractions** and answer the questions.

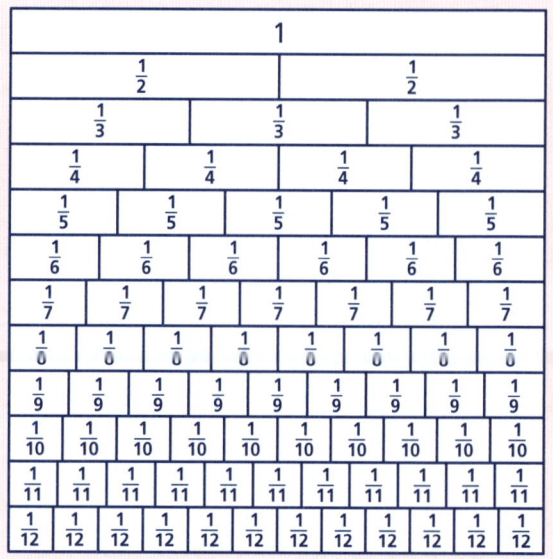

Get started

1 How many sixths are equivalent to $\frac{1}{3}$?

____2____ sixths

2 How many tenths are equivalent to one-half?

$\frac{1}{2} = \frac{5}{10}$

3 How many eighths are equivalent to one-quarter?

____2____ eighths

4 $\frac{3}{4}$ is equivalent to $\frac{6}{8}$.

5 How many lots of $\frac{1}{12}$ are equivalent to one whole? ____12____

6 The fraction $\frac{8}{10}$ is equivalent to how many fifths? ____4____ fifths

7 $\frac{2}{3} = \frac{4}{6}$

8 True or false? $\frac{3}{4} = \frac{9}{12}$

True ✓   False ☐

Now try these

9 What number is missing? $\frac{1}{2}$ is equivalent to $\frac{6}{12}$.

10 Fill the gaps with the digits 6 and 2 to create two equivalent fractions. $\frac{1}{2} = \frac{3}{6}$

11 For each diagram write the fraction of the shape that is red.

a) 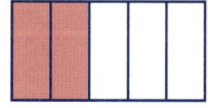 $\frac{2}{5}$

b) 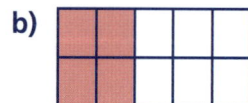 $\frac{4}{10}$ or $\frac{2}{5}$

c) 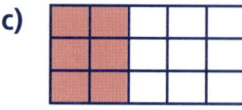 $\frac{6}{15}$ or $\frac{2}{5}$

54

Fractions, Decimals and Percentages

12. A bar of chocolate has 10 chunks. Maddie eats three-fifths of the whole bar. How many chunks does she eat? __6__

13. A large pie is cut into 12 equal slices. Jun eats two-thirds of the pie. How many slices does he eat? __8__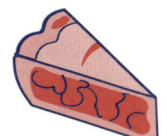

14. True or false? $\frac{2}{10} = \frac{4}{5}$ True ☐   False ✓

15. Ten out of twelve flowers in a bunch are yellow. Alice says that five-sixths of the flowers are yellow. Is she correct?   Yes ✓   No ☐

16. Find out if $\frac{4}{9}$ is greater than, less than or equivalent to $\frac{1}{3}$ by using a fraction wall.

__greater than__

Challenge

17. Harry has 9 cupcakes. $\frac{1}{3}$ are chocolate and $\frac{3}{9}$ are vanilla. Does he have more, fewer or the same number of chocolate cupcakes as vanilla cupcakes? __the same number__

18. In a sports team $\frac{8}{12}$ are girls. How many thirds of the team are girls? __2__ thirds

19. A wall is covered in tiles. $\frac{2}{6}$ of the tiles are black. $\frac{4}{12}$ of the tiles are white.
Are there the same number of black tiles as white tiles?   Yes ✓   No ☐

20. True or false? These three fractions are all equivalent: $\frac{3}{4}$ $\frac{6}{8}$ $\frac{8}{12}$ True ☐   False ✓

21. This grid has 24 squares. Joel colours 18 squares.
He then says that $\frac{3}{4}$ is equivalent to $\frac{18}{24}$. Is he correct?
Yes ✓   No ☐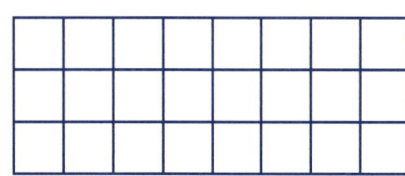

22. Is it possible to fill the gaps of this statement with odd numbers so that it is true?

$\frac{?}{12}$ is equivalent to $\frac{?}{3}$.   Yes ☐   No ✓

23. Iqra has found out that you can multiply the numerator and denominator of a fraction by the same number to get an equivalent fraction.
Multiply the numerator and denominator of $\frac{3}{4}$ by 5 to get an equivalent fraction. $\frac{15}{20}$

24. Write the equivalent fraction produced by multiplying the numerator and denominator of $\frac{2}{3}$ by 8. $\frac{16}{24}$

ANSWERS UNIT 5

Use patterns within families of equivalent fractions

Key point

Fractions with the same value are **equivalent**. This **family** of fractions is equivalent to one-half ($\frac{1}{2}$).

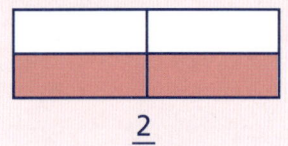 $\frac{2}{4}$ 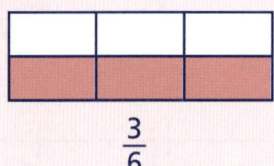 $\frac{3}{6}$ 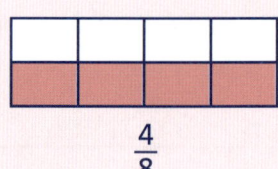 $\frac{4}{8}$ 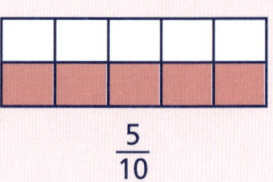 $\frac{5}{10}$

If you multiply or divide the numerator and denominator of a fraction **by the same number** you will get an equivalent fraction.

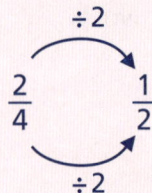 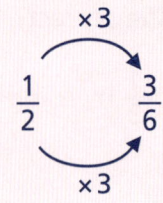 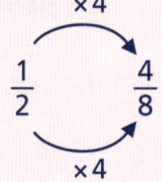 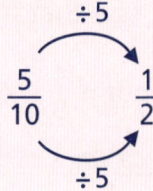

Get started

1 What is the missing equivalent fraction? $\frac{3}{4} \xrightarrow{\times 2} \frac{6}{8}$

2 Find the equivalent fraction. $\frac{3}{4} \xrightarrow{\times 5} \frac{15}{20}$

3 What is missing? $\frac{9}{12} \xrightarrow{\div 3} \frac{3}{4}$

4 What number has the numerator and denominator of two-fifths been multiplied by to give the equivalent fraction four-tenths? $\frac{2}{5} \xrightarrow{\times \boxed{2}} \frac{4}{10}$

5 The numerator and denominator of $\frac{2}{3}$ are multiplied by 4 to give what equivalent fraction? $\frac{8}{12}$

6 The numerator and denominator of $\frac{5}{15}$ are divided by 5 to give what equivalent fraction? $\frac{1}{3}$

7 Multiply both numbers of the fraction $\frac{5}{6}$ by 2 to give an equivalent fraction. $\frac{10}{12}$

8 What number have both numbers of the first fraction been divided by to give the equivalent fraction? $\frac{21}{30} \xrightarrow{\div \boxed{3}} \frac{7}{10}$

Now try these

9 True or false? $\frac{3}{5} = \frac{9}{15}$

True ✓ False ☐

10 What is the missing number? $\frac{2}{3}$ is equivalent to $\frac{6}{9}$.

Fractions, Decimals and Percentages

11 True or false? These fractions are all equivalent: $\frac{2}{8} = \frac{1}{4} = \frac{3}{12}$ True ✓   False ☐

12 Circle the fraction that is equivalent to $\frac{2}{5}$.

$\frac{1}{10}$ $\frac{2}{10}$ $\frac{3}{10}$ $(\frac{4}{10})$ $\frac{5}{10}$

13 Complete the equivalent fractions. $\frac{1}{2} = \frac{5}{10} = \frac{6}{12}$

14 Matthew says that $\frac{2}{3}$ is equivalent to $\frac{200}{300}$. Is he correct?   Yes ✓   No ☐

15 Is $\frac{30}{40}$ equivalent to $\frac{9}{12}$? $\frac{30}{40} \xrightarrow{\div ?} \frac{3}{4} \xrightarrow{\times ?} \frac{9}{12}$ Yes ✓   No ☐

16 Natasha says that $\frac{2}{4}$ is not equivalent to $\frac{3}{6}$. Is she correct?   Yes ☐   No ✓

Challenge

17 15 of these 18 stars are red. The stars are grouped into sixths.

How many sixths are red? $\frac{15}{18} = \frac{5}{6}$

18 Write a fraction equivalent to $\frac{1}{3}$ with the denominator 15. $\frac{5}{15}$

19 The 12 buttons below have been grouped in different ways.
Write three equivalent fractions to show what fraction of them are white.

a) $\frac{4}{12}$ b) $\frac{2}{6}$ c) $\frac{1}{3}$

20 Complete this pattern. $\frac{1}{3} = \frac{2}{6} = \frac{4}{12}$

21 Circle the fraction that is not equivalent to the others. $\frac{1}{5}$ $\frac{2}{10}$ $\frac{3}{15}$ $\frac{4}{20}$ $(\frac{5}{30})$

22 Ffion notices that $\frac{3}{8}$ of some counters are blue.
If there are 9 blue counters, how many counters are there in total?   24

23 There are 32 people on a bus. If $\frac{3}{8}$ of the people
are male, how many people on the bus are male?   12

24 A grid of 24 squares has 16 coloured green. What proportion
of the squares are green? Give your answer as a fraction with the numerator 2. $\frac{2}{3}$

57

ANSWERS UNIT 6

Add and subtract fractions with the same denominator

Key point

When adding or subtracting fractions, if the denominators are the same, **add or subtract the numerators only**.
The denominator stays the same.

numerator →
denominator → $\dfrac{3}{10} + \dfrac{6}{10} = \dfrac{9}{10}$ $\dfrac{9}{10} - \dfrac{6}{10} = \dfrac{3}{10}$

Some answers may be greater than 1. These answers can be given as an **improper fraction** (top-heavy fraction) or as a **mixed number** (a whole number and a fraction).

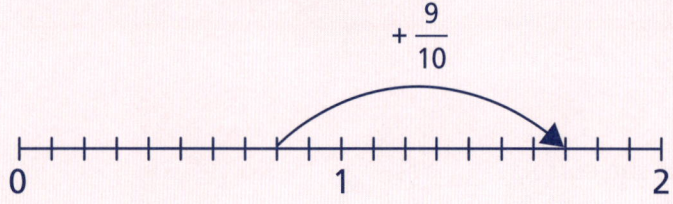

improper fraction   mixed number

$\dfrac{8}{10} + \dfrac{9}{10} = \dfrac{17}{10} = 1\dfrac{7}{10}$

Get started

1. $\dfrac{2}{9} + \dfrac{3}{9} = \boxed{\dfrac{5}{9}}$

2. $\dfrac{7}{10} + \dfrac{6}{10} = \boxed{\dfrac{13}{10}}$

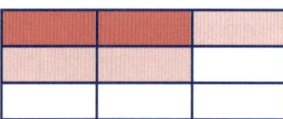

3. $\dfrac{6}{7} - \dfrac{3}{7} = \boxed{\dfrac{3}{7}}$

4. $\dfrac{8}{10} - \dfrac{3}{10} = \boxed{\dfrac{5}{10}}$

5. $\dfrac{2}{4} + \dfrac{3}{4} = \boxed{\dfrac{5}{4}}$

6. $\boxed{\dfrac{7}{9}} + \dfrac{3}{9} = \dfrac{10}{9}$

7. $\dfrac{11}{12} - \boxed{\dfrac{7}{12}} = \dfrac{4}{12}$

8. $\dfrac{3}{8} + \dfrac{1}{8} + \dfrac{3}{8} = \boxed{\dfrac{7}{8}}$

Now try these

9. Add $\dfrac{2}{5}$ to $\dfrac{4}{5}$. Give your answer as a mixed number. $1\dfrac{1}{5}$

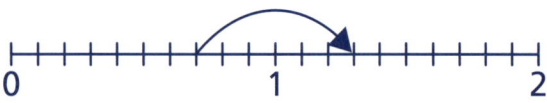

10. Subtract $\dfrac{3}{8}$ from $\dfrac{7}{8}$. Give your answer as an equivalent fraction with the numerator 1. $\dfrac{1}{2}$

11. How many sevenths is the answer to five-sevenths plus four-sevenths? 9 sevenths

12. Find the values of *a* and *b*. $\dfrac{8}{10} - \dfrac{3}{10} = \dfrac{a}{10} = \dfrac{1}{b}$ *a* = 5   *b* = 2

13. Give the sum of five-sixths and two-sixths as a mixed number. $1\frac{1}{6}$

14. Give the sum of four-ninths, five-ninths and four-ninths as an improper fraction. $\frac{13}{9}$

15. Decrease $\frac{7}{8}$ by $\frac{2}{8}$. $\frac{5}{8}$

16. | $\frac{7}{12}$ | $\frac{5}{12}$ | $\frac{9}{12}$ | $\frac{4}{12}$ | $\frac{11}{12}$ |

    Look at the fractions above. What is the largest fraction minus the smallest fraction? $\frac{7}{12}$

Challenge

17. In a litter of puppies, $\frac{1}{5}$ are black, $\frac{2}{5}$ are golden and the rest are brown. What fraction of the puppies are brown? $\frac{2}{5}$

18. Write the answer to $\frac{6}{5} + \frac{4}{5} - \frac{2}{5}$ as an improper fraction and as a mixed number.

    $\frac{8}{5}$ and $1\frac{3}{5}$

19. A bag of flour weighs $\frac{9}{10}$ kg. Ben uses $\frac{7}{10}$ kg of the flour to make a batter.

    a) What fraction of a kilogram is left? $\frac{2}{10}$ or $\frac{1}{5}$ kg
    b) How many grams is this? 200 g

20. When $\frac{8}{10}$ m is added to $\frac{6}{10}$ m, what fraction of a metre more than 1 whole metre is the result? $\frac{4}{10}$ or $\frac{2}{5}$ m

21. Adam and Ruben buy two pizzas. Each eats $\frac{5}{8}$ of a pizza. If each pizza is cut equally into eight slices, what is the total number of slices not eaten? 6

22. $\frac{5}{15} = \frac{1}{3}$ Use this fact to help you find the difference between $\frac{12}{15}$ and $\frac{1}{3}$. $\frac{7}{15}$

23. $\frac{21}{24} = \frac{7}{8}$ Use this fact to help you find the sum of $\frac{7}{8}$ and $\frac{15}{24}$.

    Give your answer as a mixed number. $1\frac{12}{24}$ Also accept $1\frac{1}{2}$

24. Poppy spent $\frac{7}{12}$ of an hour watching a cartoon and $\frac{6}{12}$ of an hour watching a quiz show.

    a) Write the total fraction of time she spent watching these, as a mixed number. $1\frac{1}{12}$ hr
    b) How many minutes is this? 65 min

ANSWERS TEST

Schofield & Sims

Check-up test 1

1 Write the fraction of this rectangle that is red.

$\frac{1}{3}$

1 mark

2 Oscar has 4 yellow t-shirts and 3 green ones in his wardrobe.
What fraction of Oscar's t-shirts are yellow?

$\frac{4}{7}$

1 mark

3 True or false? If the denominator of a fraction is larger than its numerator the fraction is greater than 1 whole.

True ☐   False ✓

1 mark

4 How many squares in $\frac{3}{4}$ of this grid? 18

1 mark

5 Colour $\frac{2}{3}$ of these snails.

1 mark

6 A centimetre is split into 10 millimetres.
What fraction of a centimetre is 3mm? $\frac{3}{10}$ cm

1 mark

7 Mark $\frac{4}{6}$ and $3\frac{1}{6}$ on this line.

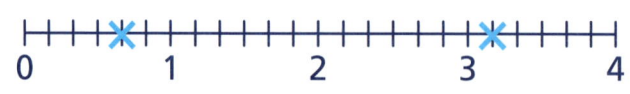

1 mark

8 What is $\frac{7}{10}$ more than $2\frac{9}{10}$?

$3\frac{6}{10}$

1 mark

9 Circle the fraction closest to the whole number 6.

$5\frac{1}{2}$ $\left(5\frac{3}{4}\right)$ $6\frac{1}{2}$ $7\frac{1}{2}$ $6\frac{3}{4}$

1 mark

10 Count back five-sixths from 2.
What mixed number do you reach? $1\frac{1}{6}$

1 mark

60

Fractions, Decimals and Percentages — Fractions 4 Teacher's Guide Test

11 How many lots of $\frac{1}{9}$ are equivalent to one whole? ___9___

1 mark

12 For each diagram, write the fraction of the shape that is red.

a)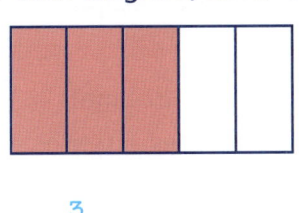

$\frac{3}{5}$

b)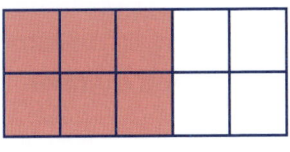

$\frac{6}{10}$ or $\frac{3}{5}$

c)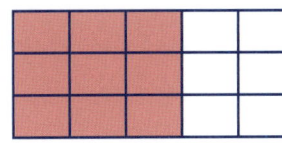

$\frac{9}{15}$ or $\frac{3}{5}$

1 mark

13 12 out of 15 pens in a pencil case are blue.

John says that three-fifths of the pens are blue. Is he correct?

Yes ☐   No ✓

1 mark

14 In a football team $\frac{9}{12}$ are girls.

How many quarters of the team are girls? ___3___ quarters

1 mark

15 Write the equivalent fraction produced by multiplying the numerator and denominator of $\frac{4}{5}$ by 6. $\frac{24}{30}$

1 mark

16 True or false? $\frac{3}{4} = \frac{9}{12}$

True ✓   False ☐

1 mark

17 Write a fraction equivalent to $\frac{1}{4}$ with the denominator 12. $\frac{3}{12}$

1 mark

18 $\frac{8}{10} - \frac{5}{10} = \boxed{\frac{3}{10}}$

1 mark

19 Subtract $\frac{5}{12}$ from $\frac{11}{12}$.

Give your answer as an equivalent fraction with the numerator 1. $\frac{1}{2}$

1 mark

20 $\frac{3}{10}$ m is added to $\frac{9}{10}$ m.

What fraction of a metre more than one whole metre is the result? ___$\frac{2}{10}$___ m

1 mark

Total

20 marks

61

ANSWERS UNIT 7   Schofield & Sims

Understand tenths as fractions and decimals

Key point

Tenths can be shown as fractions and decimals. The column to the right of the **decimal point** is the tenths column.

tenths	fraction or mixed number	decimal ones . tenths
	$\frac{1}{10}$	0 . 1
	$\frac{2}{10}$	0 . 2
	$\frac{5}{10}$	0 . 5
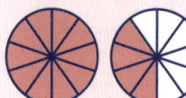	$1\frac{4}{10}$	1 . 4

Get started

1 Write as a decimal how much of this rectangle is red.
   __0.3__

2 Write 0.7 as a fraction. __$\frac{7}{10}$__

3 How many tenths are there in 0.5?
   __5__ tenths

4 What is the missing number?
   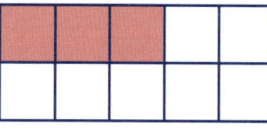
   __9__ tenths = $\frac{9}{10}$

5 Write eight-tenths as a decimal and as a fraction.
   __0.8__ and __$\frac{8}{10}$__

6 How many tenths more is 0.8 than $\frac{6}{10}$?
   __2__ tenths

7 Write what the arrow is pointing to as a decimal. __0.3__
   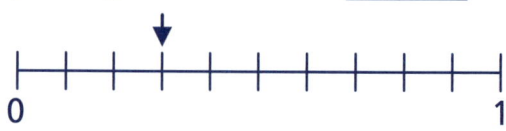

8 Colour 0.5 of this circle.
   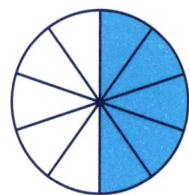

Now try these

9 A chocolate bar has 10 equal chunks.
Write as a decimal how much of the bar is six chunks. __0.6__

62

Fractions, Decimals and Percentages

10. True or false? 0.5 is equivalent to $\frac{1}{2}$. True ✓ False ☐

11. True or false? 1.2 is equivalent to the mixed number $1\frac{2}{10}$. True ✓ False ☐

12. Write $2\frac{7}{10}$ as a decimal. __2.7__

13. True or false? 2.9kg is one-tenth of a kilogram less than 3 whole kilograms. True ✓ False ☐

14. Write the missing numbers. 5.3 = | 5 | ones + | 3 | tenths

15. Continue the sequence. 0.6, 0.7, 0.8, 0.9, __1.0 or 1__, __1.1__

16. Mark 2.4cm on this ruler.

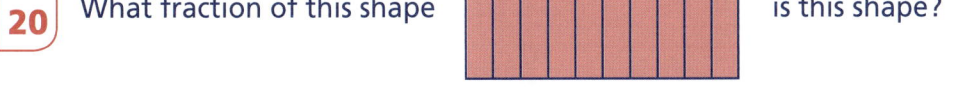

Challenge

17. Write the missing numbers. 17.6 = | 1 | ten + | 7 | ones + | 6 | tenths

18. A line of 10 square tiles measures 9m.
    a) How long is each tile, as a fraction of a metre? __$\frac{9}{10}$__ m
    b) What is this length as a decimal? __0.9__ m

19. Ten identical books weigh 8kg in total.
    What does one book weigh, written as a decimal? __0.8__ kg

20. What fraction of this shape ▬▬▬▬▬ is this shape? ▬
    Write your answer as a fraction and as a decimal. __$\frac{1}{10}$__ and __0.1__

21. 6.5 litres can be written as $6\frac{5}{10}$ litres or $6\frac{1}{?}$ litres. What is the missing number? __2__

22. A bag of sugar is 2kg. Each jar holds 0.2kg of sugar.
    How many jars are needed for all the sugar? __10__

23. A class of 30 pupils get into 10 equal groups with 3 children in each group.
    What proportion of the class are 6 of the children? Write your answer as a decimal. __0.2__

24. In a bunch of 20 flowers, 4 are blue, 10 are white and the rest are red. As a decimal, what proportion of all the flowers are red? __0.3__

ANSWERS UNIT 8   Schofield & Sims

Find decimals with one decimal place on a number line

Key point

Tenths **less than** one whole can be written as fractions or as decimals.

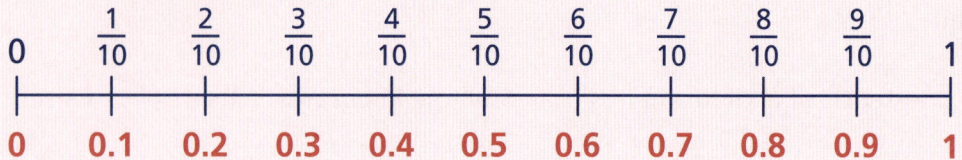

Tenths **greater than** one whole can be written as mixed numbers, improper fractions or decimals. The arrow points to $1\frac{7}{10}$ or 1.7.

Get started

1 What decimal is marked with an arrow? __0.3__

2 Continue the sequence.
1.7, 1.8, 1.9, 2, __2.1__, __2.2__

3 What is one-tenth more than $\frac{8}{10}$ as a decimal? __0.9__

4 What decimal is two-tenths less than one whole? __0.8__

5 How many tenths of a metre make 1 whole metre? __10__ tenths

6 Write the next number in the sequence, as a fraction and as a decimal.
$3\frac{6}{10}$, $3\frac{7}{10}$, $3\frac{8}{10}$, __$3\frac{9}{10}$__ or __3.9__

7 Mark 0.5 and 1.4 on this line.

8 How many tenths of a metre make:
a) $\frac{1}{2}$ a metre? __5__ tenths
b) two whole metres? __20__ tenths

Now try these

9 Which decimal (with one digit after the decimal point) lies between 2.6 and 2.8? __2.7__

10 What digit is missing to give the mass shown? 8.__6__ kg

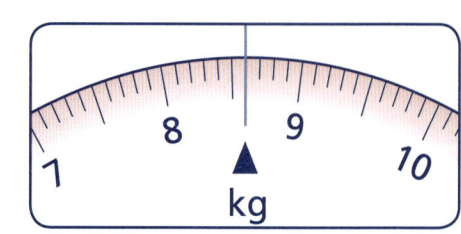

64

Fractions, Decimals and Percentages   Fractions 4 Teacher's Guide   Unit 8

11 Write these decimals in order from smallest to largest.

  5.1   5.3   5.2   5.4   __5.1__   __5.2__   __5.3__   __5.4__

12 Write the mixed number $4\frac{1}{10}$ as a decimal.   __4.1__

13 True or false? 1.2 is two-tenths larger than 0.9.

  True ☐   False ✓

14 True or false? 14 tenths is the same as 1.4.

  True ✓   False ☐

15 Write the mixed number $2\frac{1}{2}$ as a decimal.   __2.5__

16 Count back six-tenths from 2. What decimal do you reach?   __1.4__

Challenge

17 A millimetre is one-tenth of a centimetre. How many millimetres is 0.6cm?   __6__ mm

18 How many millimetres is 1.9cm?   __19__ mm

19 Mark the decimals 0.7, 1.7 and 2.7 on the line.

20 How many tenths is the difference between one whole and 0.6?   __4__ tenths

21 Some square tiles have sides that are each one-tenth of a metre. How long is a line of 13 touching tiles, in metres? Give your answer as a decimal.   __1.3__ m

22 Write the missing decimals in this sequence.

  1.5, __1.4__, 1.3, 1.2, __1.1__, 1

23 A tap drips 0.1 litre of water every minute. How many litres will it drip in 30 minutes?   __3__ l

24 Jade ran a race in 10.5 seconds. Isla took seven-tenths of a second longer.

  How long did Isla take?

  __11.2__ sec

65

ANSWERS UNIT 9   Schofield & Sims

Order and round decimals with one decimal place

Key point

The **blue** line is **0.9cm** long.
The nearest whole centimetre to 0.9cm is 1cm.
0.9 rounded to the nearest whole number is **1**.

The **red** line is **2.3cm** long.
The nearest whole centimetre to 2.3cm is 2cm.
2.3 rounded to the nearest whole number is **2**.

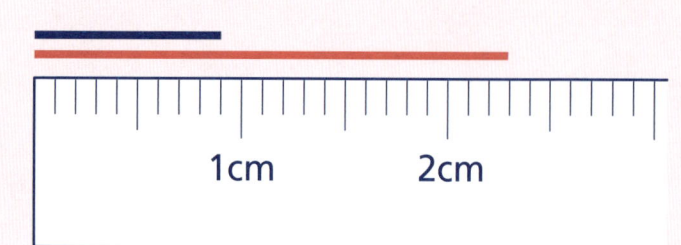

If a number is **halfway** between two whole numbers (when the tenths digit is 5), **round up**.
3.5 rounds up to 4.

2.3 > 0.9 means 2.3 is **greater than** 0.9.

Get started

1 Mark 0.7 on this number line.

2 Is 0.7 nearer to 0 or 1? ____1____

3 Circle which is greater. (0.7) 0.2

4 Which whole number is 3.8 closest to: 3 or 4? ____4____

5 Which is greater: 1.4 or 4.1? ____4.1____

6 Circle the shorter length. (2.9cm) 3.1cm

7 Is 4.5kg more or less than 5kg? ____less____

8 Round 1.6 to the nearest whole number. ____2____

Now try these

9 True or false? 1.0 is smaller than 0.9.   True ☐   False ✓

10 Use the < or > sign to show which is larger.   2.4 < 4.2

11 If you like chocolate, would you prefer to be given 2.3 bars or 1.8 bars?
____2.3____

12 What is 6.5kg rounded to the nearest whole kilogram? ____7____ kg

13 Round 10.3 to the nearest whole number. ____10____

14 True or false?   9.9 < 10   True ✓   False ☐

66

Fractions, Decimals and Percentages Fractions 4 Teacher's Guide Unit 9

15 Write the length of the line to the nearest centimetre.

___3___ cm

16 Put these decimals in order from smallest to largest.

2.4   3.1   1.9   __1.9__   __2.4__   __3.1__

Challenge

17 David is 0.8m tall. His brother is 1.1m tall. Is David taller or shorter than his brother?

_____shorter_____

18 Some athletes are doing the long jump.
Their distances jumped are shown:

Seb 4.1m   Max 2.8m   Joel 3.2m   Ali 3.8m

Which two athletes' jumps are 4 metres when rounded to the nearest whole metre?

_____Seb_____ and _____Ali_____

19 Put the above jumps in order from smallest to largest.

__2.8__ m   __3.2__ m   __3.8__ m   __4.1__ m

20 Circle all the decimals that round to 6 when rounded to the nearest whole number.

4.9   3.6   6.7   (5.5)   4.6   (6.4)   (6.1)   0.6

21 14 tenths is the same as 1 whole and 4 tenths. How is 14 tenths written as a decimal?

__1.4__

22 What is the smallest decimal with one decimal place (one digit after the decimal point) that is 3 when rounded to the nearest whole number?

__2.5__

23 Hafsa throws a beanbag 4.3m. Milly throws another beanbag 5.3m. How much further does Milly's beanbag travel? __1__ m

24 A camera takes a photo every tenth of a second. How many photos are taken in 1.3 seconds?

__13__

ANSWERS UNIT 10 — Schofield & Sims

Divide one-digit numbers by 10

Key point

When one pie is shared equally between 10 people each person gets one-tenth.
When two pies are shared equally between 10 people each person gets two-tenths, and so on.

 $1 \div 10 = \frac{1}{10} = 0.1$   $2 \div 10 = \frac{2}{10} = 0.2$

If you are giving answers as decimals, you can use **place value** when dividing by **10**. Just move the digits of the number one place to the right.

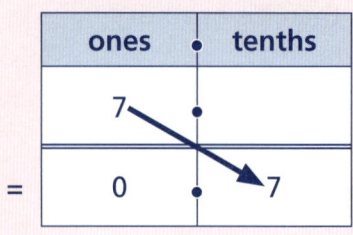

÷ 10

= zero point seven

Get started

1 $4 \div 10 =$ **0.4**

2 $7 \div 10 = \frac{7}{10} = 0.7$

3 What is nine divided by ten, as a decimal? **0.9**

4 **3** ÷ 10 = 0.3

5 What is 2 tubs of ice cream shared between 10, as a decimal? **0.2**

6 What number when divided by 10 gives 0.6? **6**

7 What decimal is the arrow pointing to? **0.3**

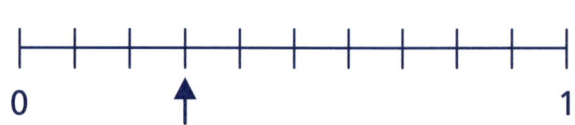

8 Four divided by ten. Write the answer in words as a decimal.
zero point four

Now try these

9 One pot of yoghurt is shared equally into ten bowls.
Write as a decimal in words how much of the pot is in each bowl.   **zero point one**

10 Nine pizzas are divided equally between ten people.

a) What fraction of a pizza does each person get? $\frac{9}{10}$

b) What is this fraction as a decimal?   **0.9**

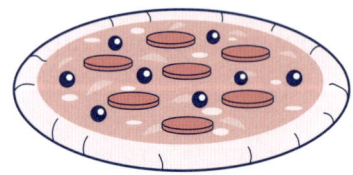

11 A farmer divides five kilograms of compost equally into 10 bags.

a) Write as a decimal how much compost is in each bag. __0.5__ kg

b) Write this as a fraction of a kilogram with the numerator 1. __$\frac{1}{2}$__ kg

12 A machine makes ten nails from a piece of metal weighing 7g.
What is the weight of each nail as a decimal if no metal is wasted? __0.7__ g

13 An 8m rope is cut into 10 equal lengths.
Write what proportion of a metre each length is as a decimal. __0.8__ m

14 Tick the longest measurement.

7cm ÷ 10 ✓ $\frac{4}{10}$ cm ☐   0.6cm ☐

15 Three litres of lemonade is poured equally into ten cups.
How much is in each cup? Give your answer as a decimal. __0.3__ l

16 Ten poles are laid touching in a line. Each is 0.6m long.
What is the length of the line? __6__ m

Challenge

17 As she walks, each of Nina's steps is 0.7m apart.
If she takes 10 steps, how far from the start has she walked? __7__ m

18 Ten buckets weigh 9kg in total. As a decimal what does one bucket weigh? __0.9__ kg

19 True or false? 10 lots of 0.4 is 4 wholes.   True ✓   False ☐

20 A line of 10 square tiles measures 5m. How long is each tile, as a decimal? __0.5__ m

21 Divide five by ten. Circle three correct answers. $\frac{1}{5}$ 0.2   0.10   ⓢ$\frac{5}{10}$ Ⓞ0.5 $\frac{1}{10}$ 0.1   Ⓞ$\frac{1}{2}$

22 $2 \div 10 = \frac{2}{10} = \frac{1}{5}$

Look at this fact. Use the fact to write $\frac{1}{5}$ as a decimal. __0.2__

23 Nathan walks from home to work and back again each day for 5 days. He walks 8km in total.
What is the distance from his home to his work, as a decimal? __0.8__ km

24 Daisy divides a number by 10 and then divides the answer by 10.
If her starting number was 60, what is her final answer? __0.6__

ANSWERS UNIT 11 — Schofield & Sims

Divide one- or two-digit numbers by 10

Key point

Any whole number can be easily divided by **10** using **place value** to give a decimal answer. Just move the digits of the number **one place to the right**.

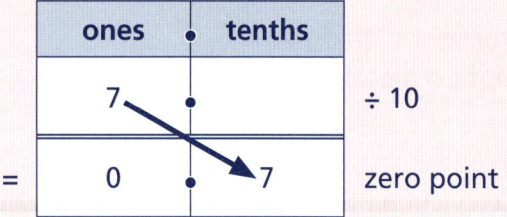

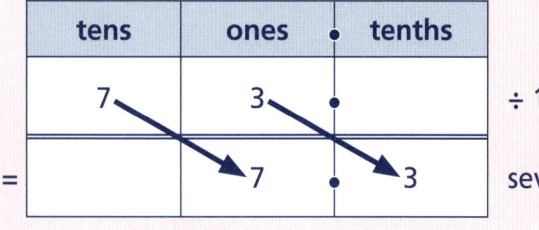

Get started

1 Divide the number in the grid by 10.

O	.	t
8	.	

__0.8__

2 Divide the number in the grid by 10.

T	O	.	t
8	3	.	

__8.3__

3 7 ÷ 10 = **0.7**

4 Write the answer to 13 ÷ 10 as a decimal. __1.3__

5 What is nineteen divided by ten, as a decimal? __1.9__

6 **35** ÷ 10 = 3.5

7 What is 12 cakes shared equally between 10, as a decimal? __1.2__

8 What number when divided by 10 gives 2.7? __27__

Now try these

9 The arrow is pointing to the answer to this question: **23** ÷ 10
What is the missing number in the question?

70

Fractions, Decimals and Percentages   Fractions 4 Teacher's Guide   Unit 11

10   A class is arranged into 10 teams. The teacher gives each team a 2.5m length of ribbon. What is the total length of all the ribbon? __25__ m

11   Mark on the line the answer to 14 divided by 10.

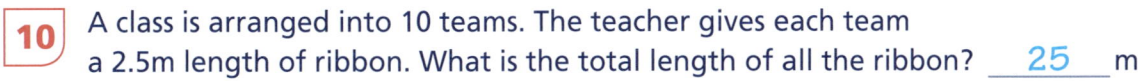

12   Divide 8 by 10. Colour parts of this whole rectangle to show the answer.

13   Divide 17 by 10. Colour parts of these whole rectangles to show the answer.

14   If 69 ÷ 10 = 6.9, what is 6.9 × 10? __69__

15   What is one-tenth of £95? £ __9.50__

16   True or false? 10 lots of 1.3 is 13 wholes.   True ✓   False ☐

Challenge

17   George says seventy divided by 10 is 7. Lauren says seventy divided by 10 is 7.0.
Who is correct? George, Lauren or both? __both__

18   A 52cm line is split into 10 equal parts. What is the length of each part:
a) in centimetres? __5.2__ cm   b) in millimetres? __52__ mm

19   True or false? 25m ÷ 10 = $2\frac{1}{2}$m   True ✓   False ☐

20   A hose lets out 3.3 litres of water every minute.
Joss wants to fill her 33-litre paddling pool.
How many minutes will it take to fill it? __10__ min

21   Hassan chooses a number to divide by ten. His answer as a mixed number is $7\frac{5}{10}$.
a) What is his answer as a decimal? __7.5__   b) What was his chosen number? __75__

22   Elena walks slowly in tiny steps across the playground, taking 78 seconds. She then runs back as fast as she can, taking one-tenth of the time. How many seconds does it take her to run back? __7.8__ sec

23   What is one-tenth of 52 plus 52? __57.2__

24   Holly has £6. She spends one-tenth of this money on a cake.
How much does she have left afterwards? £ __5.40__

71

ANSWERS UNIT 12

Understand fractions and decimals as the result of division

Key point

When a number is divided by another, the answer can be written as a fraction.
3 cakes are shared equally between 8 people. Each cake can be split into eighths.
Each person can have $\frac{1}{8}$ of each cake, so each person has $\frac{3}{8}$ altogether.

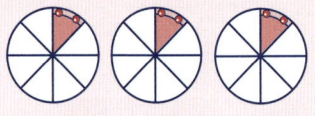

$3 \div 8 = \frac{3}{8}$ **Notice the numerator and denominator.**

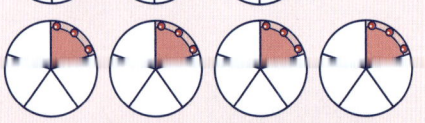

$4 \div 5 = \frac{4}{5}$

The number being divided becomes the numerator and the number being divided by becomes the denominator.

If dividing by 10, the answer can also be written as a decimal. $3 \div 10 = \frac{3}{10} = 0.3$

Get started

1 These three cakes are shared equally between four children. How much does each child get? $\underline{\frac{3}{4}}$

2 Write the answer to $1 \div 2$ as a fraction. $\underline{\frac{1}{2}}$

3 Divide 3 by 7 and give your answer as a fraction. $\underline{\frac{3}{7}}$

4 $4 \div 5 = \boxed{\frac{4}{5}}$

5 A whole number is divided by 6 to give the answer $\frac{5}{6}$. What is the whole number? $\underline{5}$

6 True or false? $7 \div 10 = \frac{7}{10} = 0.7$
True ✓   False ☐

7 Write the answer to 8 divided by 10 as a decimal. $\underline{0.8}$

8 A whole number divided by 10 gives the answer 0.4. What is the whole number? $\underline{4}$

Now try these

9 Five doughnuts are equally shared between eight people. What fraction of a doughnut does each person get? $\underline{\frac{5}{8}}$

10 Two litres of juice is poured equally into nine empty cups. What fraction of a litre is in each cup? $\underline{\frac{2}{9}}$ l

11 Mark the answer to $7 \div 8$ on this line.

(mark at $\frac{7}{8}$ between 0 and 1)

Fractions, Decimals and Percentages Fractions 4 Teacher's Guide Unit 12

12 Give the answer to 9 ÷ 10 as a fraction and as a decimal. $\frac{9}{10}$ and   0.9

13 Six TV adverts are all the same length of time. If they take 5 minutes in total to show on TV, what fraction of a minute is each advert? $\frac{5}{6}$ min

14 A 2m roll of ribbon is cut into 10 equal lengths. Write, as a decimal, the length of each.   0.2 m

15 True or false? 5 ÷ 10 and 1 ÷ 2 have the same answer when written as a decimal.

True ✓   False ☐

16 Fill in the missing numbers.   6 ÷ 8 = $\frac{6}{8}$ = $\frac{3}{4}$

Challenge

17 Peter says that £6 divided by 10 is £0.60. Is he correct?

Yes ✓   No ☐

18 Four identical display boards in a school hall are equally shared between eight classes. Write two equivalent fractions to show what fraction of a board each class has.

  $\frac{4}{8}$ and $\frac{1}{2}$

19 Thomas spends one-tenth of £7 on sweets.

a) What fraction of a pound does he spend? $\frac{7}{10}$

b) What is this as a decimal?   0.7   Also accept 0.70

20 A jug holds 2 litres of water. The water is poured into 10 cups.

a) What fraction of a litre of water does each cup hold? $\frac{2}{10}$ l

b) What is this as a decimal?   0.2 l

21 What fraction of a metre is each part when a 3m plank is sawn into 10 equal parts?

Give your answer as a fraction and as a decimal. $\frac{3}{10}$ m   and   0.3 m

22 7m ÷ 10 equals how many centimetres?   70 cm

23 If 3 pies shared between 7 equals $\frac{3}{7}$, what do 10 pies shared between 7 equal? $\frac{10}{7}$ Also accept $1\frac{3}{7}$

24 What is 17 divided by 10 as a mixed number and as a decimal? $1\frac{7}{10}$ and   1.7

73

Check-up test 2

1 How much of this rectangle is red? Write your answer as a decimal. __0.6__

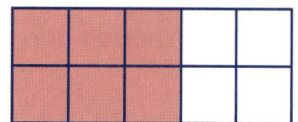

2 A chocolate bar has 10 equal chunks. Write, as a decimal, how much of the bar is 5 chunks. __0.5__

3 A bag of sand weighs 3kg. Each tub holds 0.3kg of sand. How many tubs are needed for all the sand? __10__

4 What decimal is three-tenths less than one whole? __0.7__

5 Which decimal (with one digit after the decimal point) lies between 3.2 and 3.4? __3.3__

6 How many millimetres is 2.4cm? __24__ mm

7 Alfie swam a race in 12.7 seconds. Emily took six-tenths of a second longer. How long did Emily take? __13.3__ sec

8 Mark 0.3 on this number line.

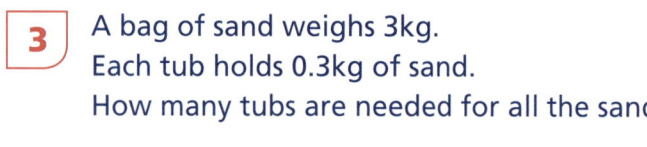

9 Circle the longer length.

1.8cm   (2.1cm)

10 Put these decimals in order from smallest to largest.

2.7   3.4   2.9   __2.7__   __2.9__   __3.4__

11 __6__ ÷ 10 = 0.6

12 Seven melons are divided between ten people.

a) What fraction of a melon does each person get? __7/10__

b) What is this fraction as a decimal? __0.7__

13 Ten boxes are placed touching in a line. Each box is 0.9m long. What is the length of the line of boxes? __9__ m

14 Niamh cycles from home to work and back again each day for 5 days. She cycles 9km in total.
What is the distance from her home to her work, as a decimal? __0.9__ km

1 mark

15 Divide the number in the grid by 10.

T	O	.	t
6	4	.	

__6.4__

1 mark

16 Jamie chooses a number to divide by ten. His answer as a mixed number is $5\frac{3}{10}$.

a) What is his answer as a decimal? __5.3__

b) What was his chosen number? __53__

1 mark

17 Divide 4 by 9 and give your answer as a fraction.

__$\frac{4}{9}$__

1 mark

18 A whole number divided by 10 gives the answer 0.7.
What is the whole number?

__7__

1 mark

19 What fraction of a metre is each part when a 4m plank is sawn into 10 equal parts? Give your answer as a fraction and as a decimal.

__$\frac{4}{10}$__ m and __0.4__ m

1 mark

20 3m ÷ 10 equals how many centimetres?

__30__ cm

1 mark

Total

20 marks

75

ANSWERS UNIT 13

Recognise hundredths as fractions and decimals

Key point

Hundredths can be shown as fractions and decimals. The column to the right of the tenths column is the hundredths column. 10 hundredths is the same as 1 tenth.

		fraction	decimal ones . tenths hundredths
	1 tenth	$\frac{1}{10}$	0 . 1
	1 hundredth	$\frac{1}{100}$	0 . 0 1
	14 hundredths	$\frac{14}{100}$	0 . 1 4
	25 hundredths	$\frac{25}{100}$ or $\frac{1}{4}$	0 . 2 5

Get started

1 How much of this whole is red? Write your answer as a decimal.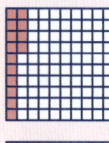
   __0.2__

2 How many tenths are there in 0.3?
   __3__ tenths

3 How much of this whole is red? Write your answer as a decimal.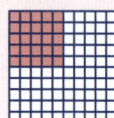
   __0.02__

4 Write the decimal 0.01 as a fraction.
   $\frac{1}{100}$

5 How many hundredths are there in 0.07?
   __7__ hundredths

6 Write nine-hundredths as a decimal and as a fraction.
   __0.09__ and $\frac{9}{100}$

7 How many hundredths more is 0.08 than $\frac{6}{100}$?
   __2__ hundredths

8 Write the next two decimals in this sequence.
   0.01, 0.02, 0.03, 0.04, __0.05__, __0.06__

Now try these

9 A toy car is $\frac{7}{100}$ m long. Write this length as a decimal.
   __0.07__ m

76

10. True or false? Ten-hundredths are the same as one-tenth.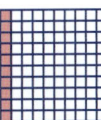

    True ✓   False ☐

11. If 14 hundredths written as a decimal is 0.14, how could you write 10 hundredths as a decimal? __0.10__ Also accept 0.1

12. What is the missing number? __13__ hundredths = $\frac{13}{100}$

13. Tick how many hundredths of this shape are red.

    34 hundredths ☐   47 hundredths ☐   43 hundredths ✓

14. $\frac{1}{4}$ of this square is red. $\frac{3}{4}$ of this square is white.

    Write $\frac{1}{4}$ and $\frac{3}{4}$ as decimals. __0.25__ and __0.75__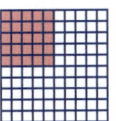

15. Colour 61 hundredths of this whole.

16. If 9 more hundredths of this whole are coloured, how many tenths would now be coloured altogether? __7__ tenths

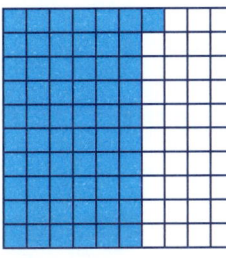

Challenge

17. Rose says that $\frac{1}{10}$ m is equivalent to $\frac{10}{100}$ m. Is she correct? Yes ✓   No ☐

18. How many tenths is the same as 30 hundredths? __3__ tenths

19. What decimal has no ones, one-tenth and seven-hundredths? __0.17__

20. True or false? $\frac{64}{100}$ = 64 hundredths = 6 tenths + 4 hundredths = 0.64   True ✓   False ☐

21. a) What fraction of a whole metre is a centimetre? __$\frac{1}{100}$__ m

    b) What is this fraction as a decimal? __0.01__ m

22. A bag of rice is 1kg. A scoop can hold 0.01kg of rice. How many full scoops of rice are in the whole bag?

    __100__

23. In a school there are exactly 100 pupils. 43 of the children are girls.

    As a decimal, what proportion of all the children are: a) girls? __0.43__   b) boys? __0.57__

24. Convert the fractions below to decimals and put them in order from smallest to largest.

    $\frac{27}{100}$ $\frac{1}{2}$ $\frac{1}{100}$ $\frac{1}{4}$ __0.01__   __0.25__   __0.27__   __0.5__

Find decimals with two decimal places on a number line

Key point

A whole split into tenths is shown on a number line with each tenth written as a fraction or a decimal. Each tenth can be split into 10 equal parts, or 10 **hundredths**.

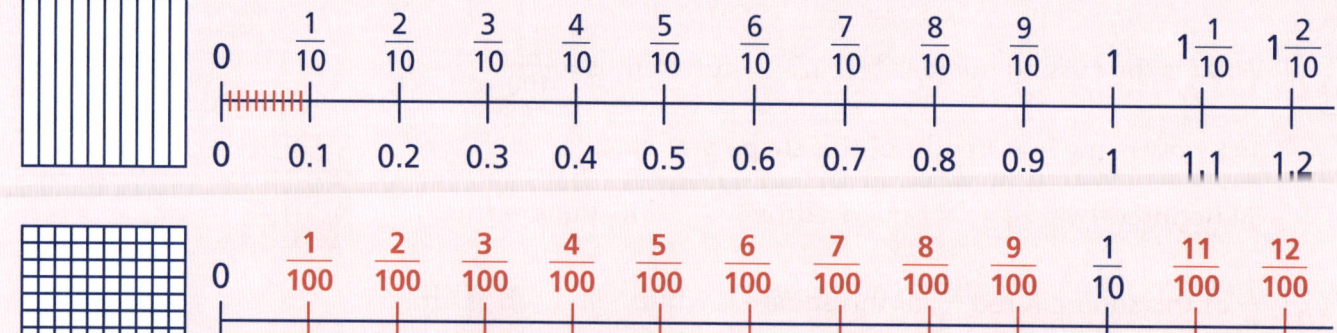

Remember:

ones	•	tenths	hundredths
0	•	1	0

=

ones	•	tenths	hundredths
0	•	1	

Get started

1 What decimal is marked with an arrow? __0.03__

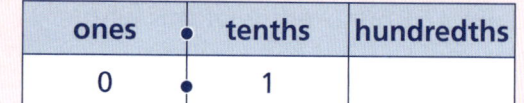

2 How many hundredths is 0.07?
__7__ hundredths

3 What is one-hundredth more than $\frac{8}{100}$ written as a decimal? __0.09__

4 Which digit is missing from this sequence?
0.08, 0.09, 0.1, 0.11, 0.__1__2, 0.13

5 Mark 0.06 and 0.14 on this line.

6 Which is smaller: 0.1 or 0.01? __0.01__

7 How many hundredths make one-tenth (or 0.1)?
__10__ hundredths

8 What decimal is two-hundredths less than 0.1? __0.08__

Now try these

9 True or false? 0.1 is the same as 0.10.   True ✓   False ☐

10 Which decimal (with two digits after the decimal point) lies between 0.14 and 0.16? __0.15__

11 Circle the three decimals that lie between 0.1 and 0.2 in this list.

0.07   (0.11)   0.25   0.63   0.4   (0.17)   0.01   (0.19)

Fractions, Decimals and Percentages   Fractions 4 Teacher's Guide   Unit 14

12 Write the two decimals marked with arrows. __0.23__ and __0.35__

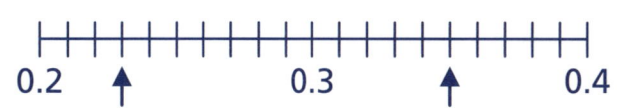

13 Luke says that 0.25 and 0.52 both lie between 0.2 and 0.3. Is he correct?

Yes ☐   No ✓

14 Which is larger: 0.29 or 0.31? __0.31__

15 Circle the decimals that do not lie between 0.4 and 0.5 in this list.

(0.53)   0.41   (0.74)   0.45   (0.63)

16 Count back six-hundredths from 0.6. What decimal do you reach?

__0.54__

Challenge

17 A centimetre is one-hundredth of a metre. How many centimetres is 0.58m? __58__ cm

18 How many centimetres is: **a)** 0.8m? __80__ cm   **b)** 0.08m? __8__ cm

19 A television camera records an image every hundredth of a second. How many images are recorded in 0.7 seconds? __70__

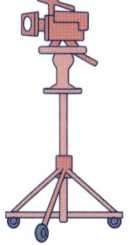

20 Write the missing decimals in this sequence.

0.85, __0.86__, 0.87, 0.88, 0.89, __0.9__, 0.91   Also accept 0.90

21 How many hundredths is the difference between 0.9 and 0.81?

__9__ hundredths

22 True or false? 0.60 is 54 hundredths greater than 0.6.   True ☐   False ✓

23 One year is one-hundredth of a century.
What proportion of a century is 17 years? Give your answer as a decimal. __0.17__

24 A dripping tap leaks 0.01 litres of water every minute.
How many litres will it drip in 24 minutes?

__0.24__ l

79

ANSWERS UNIT 15

Schofield & Sims

Compare and order decimals with two decimal places

Key point

The digits after the decimal point are called **decimal places**.
Numbers like 0.54 and 1.27 are decimals with two decimal places.

	fraction	decimal
		ones . tenths hundredths
2 hundredths	$\frac{2}{100}$	0 . 0 2
14 hundredths	$\frac{14}{100}$	0 . 1 4
113 hundredths	$\frac{113}{100}$	1 . 1 3

Get started

1 What numbers are missing?

__21__ hundredths = 0.21

__12__ hundredths = 0.12

2 Circle which is more.

(0.21)   0.12

3 How many hundredths is 1.26?

__126__ hundredths

4 How many hundredths more is 0.19 than 0.14? __5__ hundredths

5 Which is greater: 0.75 or 0.57? __0.75__

6 Which is the shorter length: 2.99cm or 3.01cm? __2.99__ cm

7 Is 0.65kg more or less than 1kg?
__less__

8 Which is more: £0.68 or £0.86?
£ __0.86__

Now try these

9 True or false? 1.90 is greater than 0.95.   True ✓   False ☐

10 How many pence more is £1.01 than £0.99? __2__ p

11 Use the < or > sign to show which is larger.   0.87 __<__ 0.93

12 Write a decimal with two decimal places that lies between 1.47 and 1.49. __1.48__

Fractions, Decimals and Percentages Fractions 4 Teacher's Guide Unit 15

13 True or false? 3.68 > 3.80   True ☐   False ✓

14 This shows part of a metre stick. The pencil is $\frac{14}{100}$ of a metre.

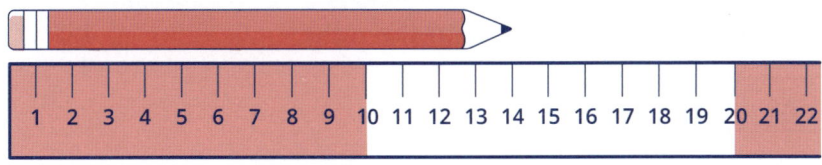

How would you write this as a decimal? __0.14__ m

15 158 hundredths is the same as 1 one, 5 tenths and 8 hundredths. How is this number written as a decimal? __1.58__

16 A centimetre is one-hundredth of a metre. How do you write 75cm in metres? __0.75__ m

Challenge

17 Put these decimals in order from smallest to largest.

0.64   0.85   0.69   __0.64__   __0.69__   __0.85__

18 Josh and Mia are growing sunflowers. Josh's sunflower is 0.84m tall. Mia's sunflower is 1.03m tall. Is Josh's sunflower taller or shorter than Mia's? __shorter__

19 Some athletes are doing the long jump. These are the lengths of their jumps:
James 3.10m   Kofi 2.87m   Dev 3.02m   Aiden 2.91m
Put their jumps in order from smallest to largest.

__2.87__ m   __2.91__ m   __3.02__ m   __3.10__ m

20 Freddie says that, because 7.5 and 7.50 are the same number, then 7.5 is larger than 7.48. Is he correct?   Yes ✓   No ☐

21 Imogen has these four cards.
Use all the cards to make a decimal with two decimal places.
What is the:

a) smallest number that can be made? __1.47__
b) largest number that can be made? __7.41__

22 What is the smallest decimal with two decimal places that is greater than 3? __3.01__

23 Rhys throws a shot-put 4.33m and Jason throws it 4.43m. How much further does Jason throw than Rhys? __0.10__ m   Also accept 0.1

24 How much smaller than £33.57 is £33.42? Give your answer in pounds. £ __0.15__

ANSWERS UNIT 16
Schofield & Sims

Divide one- or two-digit numbers by 100

Key point

Any whole number can be easily divided by **100** using **place value** to give a decimal answer. To divide by 100, move the digits of the number **two places to the right**.

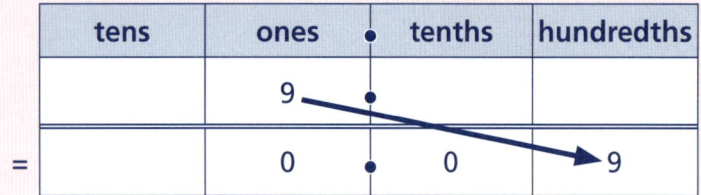

÷ 100

zero point zero nine

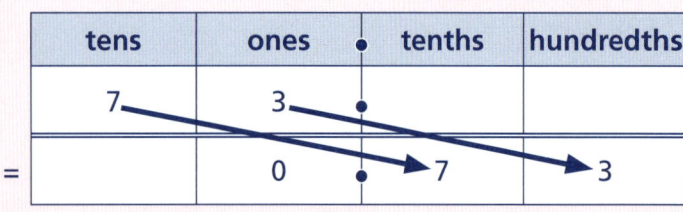

÷ 100

zero point seven three

Get started

1 Divide the number in the grid by 100.

O	.	t	h
8	.		

_0.08_

2 Divide the number in the grid by 100.

T	O	.	t	h
9	4	.		

_0.94_

3 6 ÷ 100 = 0._06_

4 Write the answer to 44 ÷ 100 as a decimal. _0.44_

5 What is 19 divided by 100 as a decimal? _0.19_

6 _26_ ÷ 100 = 0.26

7 What is 45kg shared equally between 100 as a decimal? _0.45_ kg

8 What number when divided by 100 gives 0.04? _4_

Now try these

9 The arrow is pointing to the answer to the question _33_ ÷ 100. What is the missing number in the question?

10 100 people must equally pay for something costing £97.

How much should they each pay? £ _0.97_

Fractions, Decimals and Percentages

11 Leo says that 5 ÷ 10 and 50 ÷ 100 have the same answer.

Is he correct? Yes ✓   No ☐

12 Divide 8 by 100 and colour part of this whole square to show the answer.

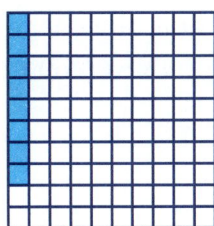

13 If 69 ÷ 100 = 0.69, what is 0.69 × 100? __69__

14 What is one-hundredth of 50 litres in litres and in millilitres?

__0.5__ l or __500__ ml   Also accept 0.50 l

15 Lexie says 900 divided by 100 is 9.00 and Noor says 900 divided by 100 is 9.

Who is correct? Lexie, Noor or both? _____both_____

16 Mark on the line the answer to 14 divided by 100.

Challenge

17 True or false? 100 lots of 0.13 is 13 wholes.   True ✓   False ☐

18 A 4m line is split into 100 equal parts. What is the length of each part:

a) in metres? __0.04__ m   b) in centimetres? __4__ cm   c) in millimetres? __40__ mm

19 Divide 130 by 100. __1.3__   Also accept 1.30

20 A hose lets out 0.33 litres of water every second.
Lara's pond holds 33 litres.
How many seconds will it take to fill the pond? __100__ sec

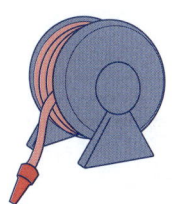

21 Hugh chooses a number to divide by 100. His answer as a mixed number is $7\frac{7}{100}$.

a) What is his answer as a decimal? __7.07__

b) What was his chosen number? __707__

22 A box containing 100 nails weighs 222 grams.
The box when empty weighs 12 grams. How much does each nail weigh? __2.1__ g

23 What is one-hundredth of 30 plus one-tenth of 30? __3.3__

24 Ella has £82. She spends one-hundredth of this money on some strawberries.

How much does she have left afterwards? £ __81.18__

ANSWERS UNIT 17

Schofield & Sims

Solve problems, including finding fractions of amounts

Key point

To find a fraction of a quantity divide by the denominator (to find one part) and multiply by the numerator (to find several parts).

numerator → 3
denominator → 10 of £50

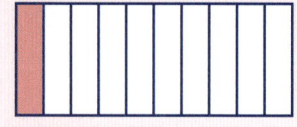

Divide the quantity by **10** to find 1 tenth.
£50 ÷ 10 = £5

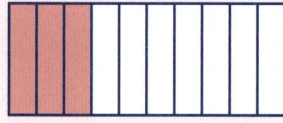

Then multiply the answer by **3** to find 3 tenths.
£5 × 3 = £15, so $\frac{3}{10}$ of £50 = £15

Get started

1. Find $\frac{1}{5}$ of 35cm. __7__ cm

2. What is two-fifths of £35? £ __14__

3. Find $\frac{7}{10}$ of 20kg. __14__ kg

4. What length is two-fifths of this line?

   0   10cm __4__ cm

5. Find $\frac{3}{4}$ of 40ml. __30__ ml

6. Find $\frac{2}{7}$ of 35cm. __10__ cm

7. Find two-thirds of 12p. __8__ p

8. Find $\frac{7}{10}$ of 40g. __28__ g

Now try these

9. A tenth of a kilogram of dog biscuits costs 15p. What does two-tenths of a kilogram cost? __30__ p

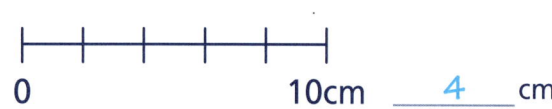

10. How many minutes in $\frac{3}{4}$ of an hour? __45__ min

11. A full turn is 360°.
    How many degrees in $\frac{2}{3}$ of a full turn? __240__ °

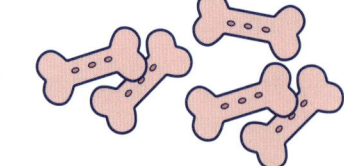

12. True or false? $\frac{4}{9}$ of 27m = 12m

    True ✓   False ☐

84

Fractions, Decimals and Percentages   Fractions 4 Teacher's Guide   Unit 17

13 Fill in the missing number.

$\boxed{\dfrac{5}{6}}$ of 12m = 10m

14 Ren takes three-quarters of the money in each box.
How much does he take in total? £ __42__

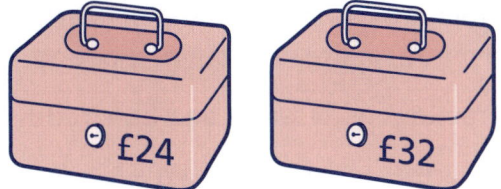

15 How many minutes is $\dfrac{5}{6}$ of an hour?

__50__ min

16 Four-sevenths of a class of 28 children wear glasses. How many children wear glasses? __16__

Challenge

17 How much less than 64cm is $\dfrac{7}{8}$ of 64cm? __8__ cm

18 A piece of ribbon is 54cm long. Sophie draws marks to divide it into nine equal parts. With scissors, she cuts once so that she has two pieces of ribbon, one with 5 of the parts and one with 4 of the parts. How long are the two pieces of ribbon?

__30__ cm and __24__ cm

19 Find the difference in kilograms between $\dfrac{3}{5}$ of 45kg and $\dfrac{5}{6}$ of 36kg. __3__ kg

20 $\boxed{\dfrac{2}{3} \text{ of £36} \quad \dfrac{5}{8} \text{ of £40} \quad \dfrac{7}{10} \text{ of £30}}$

Look at the fractions above. What is the value of: **a)** the largest of these amounts? £ __25__

b) the smallest of these amounts? £ __21__

21 Curtis is $\dfrac{7}{9}$ the height of his brother. His brother is 108cm tall.

a) How tall is Curtis? __84__ cm

b) How many centimetres taller than Curtis is his brother? __24__ cm

22 One-twelfth of an hour is 5 minutes.
What fraction of an hour is 55 minutes? __$\dfrac{11}{12}$__ hr

23 The length of a rectangle is 16cm. Its width is three-eighths of its length.
Find the perimeter of the rectangle. __44__ cm

24 Seventeen-hundredths = $\dfrac{17}{100}$ = 0.17. What is seventeen-hundredths of £200? £ __34__

85

ANSWERS UNIT 18 — Schofield & Sims

Solve problems with money and measures

Key point

Fractions can be used to show parts of a whole unit of measurement or money such as a kilogram, a metre, a litre, an hour or a pound.

Fractions with tenths and hundredths can also be shown as decimals.

$5\frac{7}{10}$ cm = **5.7** cm $\frac{13}{100}$ kg = **0.13** kg $9\frac{8}{100}$ ml = **9.08** ml

Get started

1 How many minutes is $\frac{1}{2}$ an hour? **30** min

2 Write $3\frac{7}{10}$ m as a decimal. **3.7** m

3 How many hundredths of a pound is £0.64? **64** hundredths

4 How many quarters of a kilogram are in $2\frac{1}{4}$ kilograms? **9** quarters

5 True or false? $3\frac{1}{100}$ kg = 3.1kg   True ☐   False ✓

6 Find three-fifths of 50cm. **30** cm

7 How many minutes is one-tenth of an hour? **6** min

8 What is one-third of 75ml? **25** ml

Now try these

9 ☐ 100cm = 1m

Use this fact to write 1cm as:

a) a fraction of a metre. $\frac{1}{100}$ m   b) a decimal. **0.01** m

10 Mark a cross on the ruler to show 2.7cm.

11 Circle the parcel with the heaviest mass.

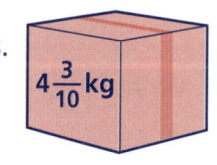 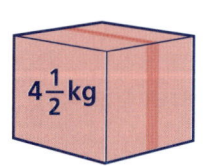 

Fractions, Decimals and Percentages

12 A 1m plank of wood is cut into 10 equal lengths.
What fraction of a metre are 7 of these lengths together? __$\frac{7}{10}$__ m

13 A garden statue is $4\frac{9}{10}$m high. The hedge beside it is $5\frac{6}{10}$m high.
How much taller is the hedge than the statue? Give your answer as a decimal. __0.7__ m

14 Sana has twenty 5p coins, making a total of £1. What fraction of one pound is:
a) 5p? __$\frac{1}{20}$__ b) 95p? __$\frac{19}{20}$__

15 Find the difference in grams between $\frac{3}{4}$ of 32g and $\frac{7}{8}$ of 24g. __3__ g

16 True or false? 60 lots of $\frac{1}{100}$kg = $\frac{60}{100}$kg = $\frac{6}{10}$kg = 0.6kg   True ✓   False ☐

Challenge

17 What is three-eighths of a litre less than 7 litres? __$6\frac{5}{8}$__ l

18 Leah puts 0.7kg of pasta into an empty bowl.
She puts the bowl and pasta on some weighing scales. The total mass is 1.2kg.
How much more does the pasta weigh than the empty bowl? __0.2__ kg

19 As she walks, each of Beth's steps is $\frac{2}{5}$m apart.
If she takes 3 steps, how far from the start has she walked?
__$1\frac{1}{5}$__ m   Also accept $\frac{6}{5}$ or 1.2m

20 Some athletes are doing the long jump.   Kate 5.1m   Abby 3.5m   Jess 4.2m   Amna 4.5m
Who jumps 4 metres when rounded to the nearest whole metre? __Abby and Jess__

21 Pippa spent three-tenths of her birthday
money on a coat. If she is left with £70,
how much was her birthday money in total? £__100__

22 Some square tiles have sides that are each $\frac{55}{100}$ of a metre.
How long is a line of 3 touching tiles, in metres?
Give your answer as a decimal. __1.65__ m

23 Evan ran a race in $10\frac{2}{5}$ seconds. Will ran it in $10\frac{4}{10}$ seconds.
What is the difference in seconds between the two times? __0__ sec

24 A machine makes 100 rings from a piece of metal weighing 80g.
What is the weight of each ring as a decimal if no metal is wasted? __0.8__ g

Check-up test 3

1 Write the decimal 0.03 as a fraction. $\frac{3}{100}$

1 mark

2 Colour 39 hundredths of this whole.

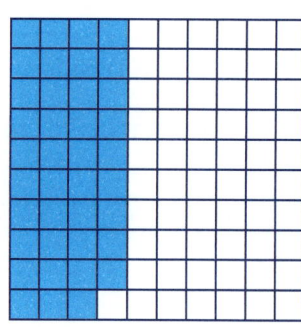

1 mark

3 What decimal has no ones, 3 tenths and 4 hundredths? __0.34__

1 mark

4 A class of 30 pupils get into 5 equal groups with 6 children in each group. Write as a decimal what proportion of the class are 12 of the children. __0.4__

1 mark

5 Mark 0.09 and 0.12 on this line.

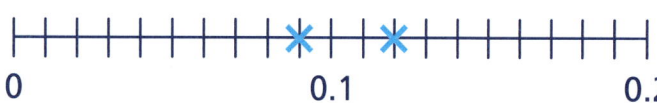

1 mark

6 Circle the three decimals that lie between 0.3 and 0.4.

0.47   0.41   (0.35)   0.61   0.4   (0.37)   (0.31)   0.29

1 mark

7 A centimetre is one-hundredth of a metre.
How many centimetres is 0.74m? __74__ cm

1 mark

8 Circle which is more.

0.34   (0.43)

1 mark

9 Use the < or > sign to show which is larger.

0.53 [<] 0.71

1 mark

10 Bailey and Domino are two donkeys at the stable.
Bailey is 1.19m tall. Domino is 0.95m tall.
Is Bailey taller or shorter than Domino? __taller__

1 mark

Fractions, Decimals and Percentages   Fractions 4 Teacher's Guide Test

11 Write the answer to 37 ÷ 100 as a decimal. __0.37__

1 mark

12 Mark on the line the answer to 26 divided by 100.

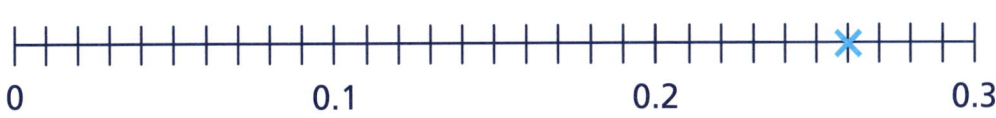

1 mark

13 Divide 170 by 100. __1.70__   Also accept 1.7

1 mark

14 Find $\frac{3}{10}$ of 30kg. __9__ kg

1 mark

15 A tenth of a kilogram of bird food costs 25p.
What does three-tenths of a kilogram cost?
__75__ p

1 mark

16 Find the difference in kilograms between $\frac{5}{8}$ of 32kg and $\frac{3}{5}$ of 30kg. __2__ kg

1 mark

17 One-twelfth of an hour is 5 minutes.
What fraction of an hour is 35 minutes? __$\frac{7}{12}$__ hr

1 mark

18 How many quarters of a kilogram are in $1\frac{3}{4}$ kilograms? __7__ quarters

1 mark

19 Mark a cross on the ruler to show 2.4cm.

1 mark

20 Some athletes are throwing the javelin.
Their throws are:
Ben 25.3m   Ava 24.5m   Ellen 25.6m   Kai 24.3m

Which athletes' throws are 25 metres when rounded to the nearest whole metre?

__Ben and Ava__

1 mark

Total

20 marks

89

Final test

Section 1

1 $\boxed{\frac{2}{3}}$ is equivalent to $\boxed{\frac{6}{9}}$.

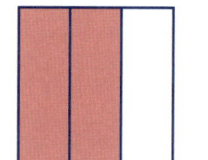 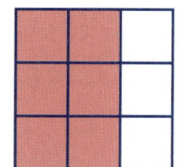

1 mark

2 For each diagram write the fraction of the shape that is red.

a) 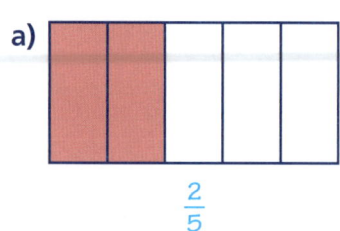 $\frac{2}{5}$

b) $\frac{4}{10}$ or $\frac{2}{5}$

c) 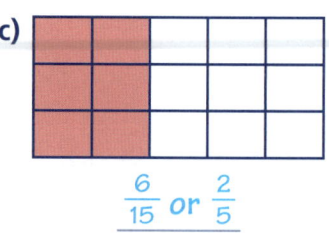 $\frac{6}{15}$ or $\frac{2}{5}$

1 mark

3 Circle any fractions that are equivalent to one-quarter.

$\frac{2}{6}$ $\left(\frac{2}{8}\right)$ $\frac{5}{12}$ $\frac{3}{9}$ $\left(\frac{3}{12}\right)$ $\left(\frac{5}{20}\right)$

1 mark

Section 2

4 How many hundredths is the same as one-tenth? __10__ hundredths

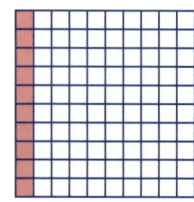

1 mark

5 Write the answer to 1 ÷ 100 as a fraction. $\frac{1}{100}$

1 mark

6 Continue this sequence. $\frac{8}{100}, \frac{9}{100}, \frac{1}{10}, \frac{11}{100}, \underline{\frac{12}{100}}, \underline{\frac{13}{100}}$

1 mark

Section 3

7 Find $\frac{3}{4}$ of £100. £ __75__

1 mark

8 Find $\frac{3}{7}$ of 35cm. __15__ cm

1 mark

9 A toy piano is 108cm tall. The stool is $\frac{5}{9}$ the height of the piano.

How tall is the stool? __60__ cm

1 mark

Section 4

10. What is five-sevenths more than three-sevenths as a mixed number? $1\frac{1}{7}$ [1 mark]

11. $\frac{3}{8} + \frac{5}{8} + \frac{5}{8} = \boxed{\frac{13}{8}}$ Also accept $1\frac{5}{8}$ [1 mark]

12. $\frac{11}{12} - \frac{4}{12} = \boxed{\frac{7}{12}}$ [1 mark]

Section 5

13. Write all these fractions as decimals.

$\frac{1}{10}$ $\frac{11}{100}$ $\frac{13}{10}$ $\frac{6}{100}$ $\frac{142}{100}$

  0.1   0.11   1.3   0.06   1.42   [1 mark]

14. True or false? $\frac{73}{100}$ = 73 hundredths = 7 tenths + 3 hundredths = 7.3

True ☐   False ✓   [1 mark]

15. Write the decimal that is 2 ones and 3 hundredths.   2.03   [1 mark]

Section 6

16. What is one-half written as a decimal?

$\frac{1}{2} = \frac{?}{10} = \boxed{0.5}$ [1 mark]

17. $\frac{1}{4}$ of this square is red. $\frac{3}{4}$ of this square is white.

Write $\frac{1}{4}$ as a decimal.   0.25   [1 mark]

18. Write $\frac{3}{4}$ as a decimal.   0.75   [1 mark]

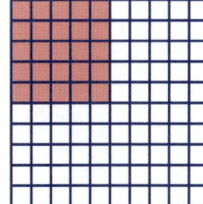

please turn over

91

Section 7

19 Answer these four questions, giving each answer as a fraction or mixed number.

7 ÷ 10 = $\frac{7}{10}$ 19 ÷ 10 = $1\frac{9}{10}$ 9 ÷ 100 = $\frac{9}{100}$ 49 ÷ 100 = $\frac{49}{100}$

1 mark

20 Answer the same four questions, giving each answer as a decimal.

7 ÷ 10 = 0.7   19 ÷ 10 = 1.9   9 ÷ 100 = 0.09   49 ÷ 100 = 0.49

1 mark

21 Circle the decimal that shows three-tenths and one-hundredth.

1.3   3.1   0.13   (0.31)   3.01

1 mark

Section 8

22 Round each decimal to the nearest whole number.

0.6 → 1   3.8 → 4   7.4 → 7   9.5 → 10   0.2 → 0

1 mark

23 Circle the decimal which, when rounded to the nearest whole number, rounds to 8.

8.8   0.8   3.8   6.5   8.5   (7.7)   9.1

1 mark

24 Write the missing digit to show the smallest decimal with one place that rounds to the nearest whole number 5.   4.5

1 mark

Section 9

25 Use either the < or > sign to show which is larger.

0.8 > 0.6   5.3 < 7.1

1 mark

26 Circle the larger decimal.   (0.73)   0.69

1 mark

27 Write these decimals from smallest to largest.

0.75   1.03   0.94   0.75   0.94   1.03

1 mark

92

Section 10

28 Iona has £69. She spends one-hundredth of this money.
How much does she have left afterwards?

£ _68.31_

1 mark

29 Kasper is 0.89m tall. His brother is 1.01m tall.
Is his brother taller or shorter than Kasper?

____taller____

1 mark

30 Mariam puts 0.9kg of flour into an empty bowl.
She puts the bowl and flour on some weighing scales.
The total mass is $1\frac{1}{10}$ kg.
How much does the empty bowl weigh?
Write your answer as a decimal.

___0.2___ kg

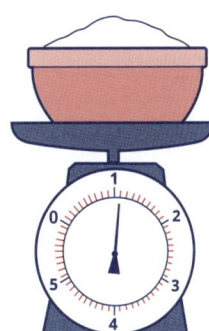

1 mark

End of test

Total

30 marks

Pupil progress chart

Pupil's name _____ Class / set _____

Unit	Get started	Now try these	Challenge	Total
1	/8	/8	/8	/24
2	/8	/8	/8	/24
3	/8	/8	/8	/24
4	/8	/8	/8	/24
5	/8	/8	/8	/24
6	/8	/8	/8	/24
Check-up test 1				/20
7	/8	/8	/8	/24
8	/8	/8	/8	/24
9	/8	/8	/8	/24
10	/8	/8	/8	/24
11	/8	/8	/8	/24
12	/8	/8	/8	/24
Check-up test 2				/20
13	/8	/8	/8	/24
14	/8	/8	/8	/24
15	/8	/8	/8	/24
16	/8	/8	/8	/24
17	/8	/8	/8	/24
18	/8	/8	/8	/24
Check-up test 3				/20

From: **Fractions 4 Teacher's Guide** © Schofield & Sims Ltd, 2017. This page may be photocopied after purchase.

Final test group record sheet

Pupil's name	Total	Y4/F1		Y4/F2			Y4/F3			Y4/F4			Y4/F5			Y4/F6			Y4/F7			Y4/F8			Y4/F9			Y4/F10		
		1	2	3	4	5	6	7	8	9	10	11	12	13	14	15	16	17	18	19	20	21	22	23	24	25	26	27	28	29	30
	/30																														

From: *Fractions 4 Teacher's Guide* © Schofield & Sims Ltd, 2017. This page may be photocopied after purchase.

SERIES LIST

Full list of books in the Fractions, Decimals and Percentages series

Pupil books

Fractions 1	ISBN 978 0 7217 1375 5
Fractions 2	ISBN 978 0 7217 1377 9
Fractions 3	ISBN 978 0 7217 1379 3
Fractions 4	ISBN 978 0 7217 1381 6
Fractions 5	ISBN 978 0 7217 1383 0
Fractions 6	ISBN 978 0 7217 1385 4

Teacher's guides

Fractions 1 Teacher's Guide	ISBN 978 0 7217 1376 2
Fractions 2 Teacher's Guide	ISBN 978 0 7217 1378 6
Fractions 3 Teacher's Guide	ISBN 978 0 7217 1380 9
Fractions 4 Teacher's Guide	ISBN 978 0 7217 1382 3
Fractions 5 Teacher's Guide	ISBN 978 0 7217 1384 7
Fractions 6 Teacher's Guide	ISBN 978 0 7217 1386 1

Free downloads available from the Schofield & Sims website

A selection of free downloads is available from the Schofield & Sims website (www.schofieldandsims.co.uk/free-downloads). These may be used to further enhance the effectiveness of the programme. The downloads add to the range of print materials supplied in the teacher's guides.

- **Graphics** slides containing the visual elements from each teacher's guide unit provided as Microsoft PowerPoint® presentations.
- **Go deeper investigations** providing additional extension material to develop problem-solving and reasoning skills.
- **Additional resources** including a fraction wall, a comparison chart and number lines to support learning and teaching.